Remember the 70s

Remember the 70s

Derek Tait

PEN & SWORD
HISTORY

First published in Great Britain in 2018 by
Pen & Sword HISTORY
An imprint of
Pen & Sword Books Ltd
47 Church Street
Barnsley
South Yorkshire
S70 2AS

Copyright © Derek Tait 2018

ISBN 978 1 47389 299 6

Printed and bound in England by CPI Group (UK) Ltd, Croydon,
CR0 4YY.

Pen & Sword Books Ltd incorporates the Imprints of
Pen & Sword Archaeology, Atlas, Aviation, Battleground, Discovery, Family
History, History, Maritime, Military, Naval, Politics, Railways, Select,
Transport, True Crime, Fiction, Frontline Books, Leo Cooper, Praetorian
Press, Seaforth Publishing, Wharncliffe and White Owl.

For a complete list of Pen & Sword titles please contact
PEN & SWORD BOOKS LIMITED
47 Church Street, Barnsley, South Yorkshire, S70 2AS, England
E-mail: enquiries@pen-and-sword.co.uk
Website: www.pen-and-sword.co.uk

Contents

Introduction

The 1970s was one of the most exciting, innovative and colourful decades of recent times. These years played a key role in British social history with major events in music, film and television as well as memorable occasions such as the Queen's Silver Jubilee and the election of the country's first female Prime Minister, Margaret Thatcher.

Red Rum won the Grand National for the third time, Manchester United won the FA Cup for the fourth time and Liverpool won their first European Cup. James Callaghan opened the M5 motorway, Kenny Dalglish became the most expensive footballer after a £440,000 transfer fee and Geoff Boycott scored the 100th century of his career. Virginia Wade won the Women's Singles at Wimbledon, Freddie Laker launched his budget Skytrain airline and Clive Sinclair launched the 2-inch television. The end of the decade also saw the five-year hunt for the 'Yorkshire Ripper', Peter Sutcliffe.

Crazy fashions included flares, platform shoes, wing-collared shirts and kipper ties. Glam rock artists such as Roy Wood, Marc Bolan, David Bowie and Bryan Ferry added to the style and dress of a generation.

Some of the best remembered films were released in the 1970s including *Star Wars, Jaws, Close Encounters of the Third Kind, Saturday Night Fever, The Godfather, Rocky, Dirty Harry* and *One Flew Over the Cuckoo's Nest*.

The 1970s also saw some of the best loved bands formed including Queen, Blondie, Slade, Wizzard, the Sex Pistols, the Damned, the Stranglers and many more.

Television shows included Charlie's Angels, Happy Days, The Six Million Dollar Man, Hawaii Five-0, M*A*S*H, The Waltons, Kojak, Rhoda, Wonder Woman, Columbo, The Rockford Files, Soap, The

Man From Atlantis, Roots and Jesus of Nazareth. The Morecambe and Wise Christmas Show in 1977 attracted 28 million viewers, one of the highest viewing figures in UK television history, while artists such as Benny Hill and Tommy Cooper were the nation's favourites.

With innovations in music, film, television, as well as social change and new technology, the 1970s was one of the most memorable decades in recent times.

Chapter 1

Home Life

At the beginning of the 1970s, Harold Wilson was the Prime Minister and Elizabeth II had been Queen since 1952. Popular television shows included Dixon of Dock Green, Z-Cars, Coronation Street, On the Buses, Opportunity Knocks, Callan and the Benny Hill Show. In 1970 chart toppers included Mungo Jerry, Edison Lighthouse, Dana, Mary Hopkin, Desmond Dekker and Cliff Richard.

At home, most families lived in rented accommodation although many, for the first time, were able to purchase property. Central heating, with radiators in every room, was a relatively new thing and all houses had single glazed, wooden-framed windows which meant in the winter months that rooms were colder and draughtier and sometimes frost would form on the inside of windows. In comparison to today, homes in 1970 were very different without most of the things that we now take for granted like double-glazing, duvets, computers to name but a few. Most homes were heated by a gas or electric fire in the front room although there were still many homes heated by coal fires and on cold winter days, the smell of chimney smoke filled the air.

Most fathers worked from 9am to 5pm and most mothers stayed at home although more and more mothers worked, to help to pay for extras such as a new mortgage, technology and family holidays.

There were several callers to the house during the day. Before 9am, the milkman, postman and paperboy had all visited. Many people had their newspapers delivered and expected to read them over breakfast before setting off to work. It was the same with the post, which was delivered twice daily by a smartly-dressed postman. The milkman arrived, in many cases, long before the family arose. He would turn up on an electric milk float stacked with milk which would be left on his customers' doorsteps ready for their morning breakfast.

Children would be sent off to school on foot giving them enough time to reach the school gates by 9am. The school day continued until around 4pm. Teachers were generally strict and the curriculum included accepted subjects such as Maths, English, Geography, History, Chemistry, Physics, Woodwork and Domestic Science (cookery).

At home, most people knew their neighbours and were on friendly terms with each other. Many still left their doors unlocked. Fewer people had cars and many residential streets were empty of vehicles allowing children space to play games of football on the road. The local policeman would patrol his beat (on foot) and, most of the time, crimes would be trivial, involving telling off children for minor misdemeanours. Most children played outside, building go-karts or dens, riding their bikes or scooters, playing games such as 'it' or hopscotch, taking part in war games or playing cowboys and Indians, happily 'shooting' their friends.

A dial phone, common in homes during the decade. These came in a variety of colours and were rented from British Telecom.

Most homes didn't have a telephone and calls had to be made from the nearest red telephone box which took pennies and halfpennies before decimalisation was introduced before the call price was changed to 2p and 10p. However, by the middle of the 1970s, more people started to get their own phones which could only be rented from the GPO. Nobody, at the time, actually owned their own phone. In some areas, there was a waiting list of six months before a phone could be fitted. There were no push buttons at the beginning of the decade and all calls had to be tediously dialled. Quite often there were crossed-lines as everyone was on a party line, meaning that the phone could sometimes pick up another person's conversation. The new home service offered 'novelty' calls such as Dial-a-Disc (where you could hear the latest pop record by dialling 16), the speaking clock, sports results and the weather. Phones came in a variety of colours including mustard, green and bright red.

The centre of the front room was no longer the fireplace but instead was the wood-surround television. Many televisions had dials to tune them in and there were no remote controls. Most televisions

A 1970s front room with brightly-coloured wallpaper and curtains.

in the early 1970s showed only black and white pictures and nearly all sets were rented from electrical stores such as DER, Rumbelows or Granada. Screens were small, in comparison to today, and if you had an 18-inch screen, you were doing well. All had tabletop aerials or an aerial on the roof and there were no satellite dishes at the time. Indoor aerials led to 'ghosting', where many images of the original could be seen. This meant that aerials had to be held up all around the room to achieve the clearest image. The problem was not properly solved until digital television was introduced. Televisions also broke down but, unlike today, a repair man came around and replaced parts and re-soldered others until the set was back to normal. The worst news you could receive is 'Your tube is going!' which meant, if you owned the set, that you'd have to buy another – a great expense in the 1970s.

Homes became much more whackily decorated in the early 1970s with the introduction of wild and wonderful wallpapers, of every colour imaginable, and more modern decor which reflected the fashions of the day. Wallpapers featuring stripes and crazy patterns, appeared everywhere. Popular colours included purple, brown, orange

A 1970s home complete with loud wallpaper, Ercol furniture, serving hatch and a 6/6 picture from Woolworths showing the rocky coast of Cornwall.

and green. Swivel chairs became popular items of furniture as did flat-packed wood-effect wall units, sometimes called 'room dividers'. Ercol, real wood, furniture was also popular. Carpets came in weird colours and wonderful patterns and shag-pile carpet became popular for a while. Curtains were also brightly coloured.

In some homes built-in fire places, complete with stick-on plastic bricks, became a feature of the front room. A burning log effect was gained by turning on a red bulb under a plastic covering showing what a fire used to look like in the days before gas. For a while, everyone wanted one.

Ornaments included heavy brightly-coloured pots, wooden carved animals, heavy glass ashtrays (everyone seemed to smoke), coloured glass vases and Mamod Steam Engine Tractors.

Pictures included sea scenes and landscapes (available from Woolworth's for 6/6) as well as string-patterns and brightly-coloured prints. Clocks reflected the age with many being made of brightly coloured plastic that came in colours such as orange, yellow or red.

Children's bedrooms were adorned with posters of pop and television stars of the day. Pace Posters were very popular and could

A boy's bedroom, complete with dark blue wallpaper, orange curtains, a portable Fidelity record player and a pile of American comics.

be bought from newsagents or specialised shops selling just posters of popular stars such as Debbie Harry, Charlie's Angels or glam rock stars.

Boys completed Airfix and Revell kits and airplanes and spaceships would hang from their bedroom ceilings. Just after the 1969 Moon landing, there was still a great interest in the space programme and toys and games reflected this. Toys such as Major Matt Mason and anything connected with the many sci-fi shows on tv were very popular. The latest games and toys included Viewmaster, Spirograph, Operation, Scalextric, football tables, Subbuteo and later early games consoles. Most boys had a magic or chemistry set. Many teenagers had their own portable record players with small collections of the latest LPs and 7-inch singles.

In the kitchen, appliances such as freezers and washing machines were still a luxury in the early 1970s. Most homes had a small fridge with a tiny freezer compartment in the top which was just big enough to take a block of ice-cream or a packet of Birdseye fish fingers. Slabs of ice-cream, which were a treat, could be bought from the local ice-cream van which toured estates bringing children out into the streets attracted by its chimes. Popular ice creams and lollies included 99s, Fab, Zoom, Haunted House, Funny Feet and Woppa. By the end of the 1970s, most households had larger, or separate, freezers. Supermarkets now stocked a huge range of frozen food. By bulk buying food, families could now save time and money by not having to travel to the local shop on a daily basis.

Ice cream, in many different flavours, could be kept at home which led, for the first time, to a range of ice cream being introduced specifically aimed at the home market. A number of freezer shops opened, the most remembered being Bejam (now Iceland). Specialist cookbooks and magazines were published explaining how to make the most of your new freezer. Other modern items found in the kitchen in the 1970s included the food blender and the fondue set. Teasmades were popular for a while and came with a clock that could be set to make a cup of tea as soon as you woke up. This seemed an excellent idea although the tea never tasted as it should and the craze soon

A Mister Softee ice cream van common on the streets of the UK during the 1970s.

died out. Breville toasters looked very appealing on television adverts and everyone had to have one. The appliance allowed you to make your own sealed toasted sandwiches which was great the first few times, but soon the novelty wore off and the machine became relegated to the back of the cupboard.

More modern kitchens featured a breakfast bar, brightly coloured kitchen cupboards and a linoleum floor in a range of colours and patterns. Most cookers were small and ran on either electric or gas. Microwave ovens began to appear towards the end of the 1970s although most families didn't own one until the 1980s.

Adverts on the television encouraged people to buy things that they didn't really need. Ronco and K–Tel produced a whole range of items including an iron so you could iron your curtains while they were up, a gadget allowing its owner to put rhinestones all over their denim jacket, record cleaning machines and the 'Dial-O-Matic' which

A boy of the 1970s complete with flared jeans, purple shirt, knitted tanktop, long hair and a 12/6 Woolworth's guitar.

sliced vegetables with ease. Many of these products came out for the Christmas market; by the end of January, most families were bored with them.

Bathrooms were also decorated with wild wallpaper, carpet on the floor and bathroom suites in a variety of strong colours including purples, browns, yellows and greens. Tiles included dark browns or brightly coloured oranges and greens as well as highly patterned designs. More modern bathrooms had radiators although many didn't, with people relying, rather dangerously, on two-bar electric fires. Walk-in showers were still unheard of in the home. Products found in the bathroom included Hai Karate and Brut 33 aftershaves, along with Cossack hairspray for men, Sunsilk for women, Old Spice and Palmolive, Lux and Cusson's Imperial Leather soaps.

By 1974 many families had bought their own colour television set and the family would gather around it to watch the latest soaps, dramas and comedies. It became the centre of the home and watching television for the first time in colour seemed an amazing experience. By the end of the 1970s the first video recorders appeared but most families didn't own

A typical wood-surround television of the decade. All came with the latest push buttons to change the channels. In the 1970s there were only three channels – BBC1, BBC2 and ITV.

one. At a cost of well over £400 most people found them too expensive. However, like televisions, video recorders could be hired.

Record players at the beginning of the 1970s were pretty basic and had one function only, to play records. There were many Dansette and other portable players available but the family record player was huge. People were amazed when a record player and radio were first combined and they were the must-have item. Eventually, they incorporated a cassette player which meant, for the first time, people could record direct from the radio or from their record collection. Previously, tape recorders had required a separate microphone to record music which meant that everyone had to keep quiet while the recording was in progress.

Cassette players were introduced in the early 1970s and were portable. They too were a must have item, especially among teenagers. Eight track cartridges were also produced at about the same time and for the first time introduced in-car pre-recorded music into people's lives.

The radio played a large part in people's lives at home and stations listened to featured the latest pop music, mainly on Radio 1, with the run down of the top 40 on Sunday afternoons with Alan 'Fluff' Freeman. The BBC and Radio Luxembourg were the most popular radio stations at the beginning of the 1970s but by the mid-1970s, local radio stations started appearing. Pocket transistor radios brought portability to music, meaning that kids could carry them anywhere. At home, clock radios were popular. It might not seem very hi-tech now but, at the time, combining a clock and a radio was a novel idea.

The 1970s saw various industrial strikes which led to the power being cut to many homes. Every housewife had a ready supply of candles in case the lights went out and people read, played board games or listened to battery operated radios until the power came back on. Many children found it an exciting adventure although they weren't too happy about missing their favourite television programmes.

Decimalisation played a big part in people's lives during 1971. The new money proved confusing to many. Posters and signs appeared everywhere explaining the new currency. Previously, the change in your pocket was heavy and caused holes in the linings of trousers. The new money was lightweight and instead of 120 pennies to the pound, there were now 100. A shilling had previously been twelve pennies but was now just five. Older people were unhappy with the new money but it was here to stay.

Families had more disposable income by the later 1970s which meant that more could be spent on luxury items, toys for the children, cars and holidays. Most holidays had previously been within the UK, visiting seaside resorts or holiday camps such as Butlins and Pontins, but now, thanks to cheap package deals, more exotic holidays were possible and families could travel further afield to places such as Spain, Malta and Portugal. However, most stuck to travelling within the UK.

In 1976 Britain was hit by a heatwave and drought that continued for many months. It's remembered as being one of the hottest and driest summers in recent history. Many people spent a lot more time outdoors enjoying the sunny weather but the ensuing drought meant

A street party celebrating the Queen's Silver Jubilee in 1977. The celebrations were held between 6 and 9 June.

that many neighbourhoods had to get their water from standpipes. However, the rain eventually came and Britain returned to its normal weather pattern.

In 1977 Britain celebrated the Queen's Silver Jubilee. Street parties were organised up and down the country and most people became wrapped up in the excitement. The Queen toured the whole country and millions of flag-waving loyal subjects turned out to see her.

Home life revolved around the front room where families came together to eat, play games or watch the television. Board games were still very popular during the 1970s and included Monopoly, Mousetrap, Battleships, Buckaroo and Ker-plunk! The joy of playing board games slowly ebbed away as video games became more and more popular.

Entertainment for dads at the weekend included watching football, visiting the pub or watching sport on television either on Grandstand or World of Sport. At 5pm the football results were broadcast when all men dreamed of striking it rich by winning the pools.

An early bulky top-loading video recorder. Early VHS tapes lasted between two and three hours.

The home changed greatly over the decade with the introduction of home computers (although nothing like the computers of today and certainly no internet), video games, video recorders, music centres, Sony Walkmans, microwaves, washing machines, dishwashers, fridge freezers and many other appliances which we all take for granted today.

Celebrity quotes:

'*Any woman who understands the problems of running a home will be nearer to understanding the problems of running a country.*' Margaret Thatcher (1979).

'*I could be a housewife... I guess I've vacuumed a couple of times.*' Debbie Harry.

'*I think Churchill would be appalled at the Thatcher government.*' Sir Edward Heath.

'*If you want something said, ask a man; if you want something done, ask a woman.*' Margaret Thatcher.

Chapter 2

Fashion

T he 1970s saw some of the most memorable fashions of the last fifty years including platform shoes, kipper ties, large wing collars, tank tops and huge flared trousers. The decade began with a hippie style left over from the 1960s which included tie-dyed T-shirts, floral blouses, ponchos, capes, military surplus wear, as well as denim bell-bottomed trousers. Frayed jeans, midi skirts and ankle-length maxi dresses were also well-loved.

Roy Wood of Wizzard with his own take on glam rock fashion.

Platform shoes were a must-have during the glam rock era. Heels got gradually bigger and bigger during the period, as did the flares on trousers.

In the early 1970s mini skirts were still incredibly popular after first being introduced in the late 1960s. For women and young girls, hot pants became fashionable in 1971.

In 1972 Joni Mitchell wore tie-dye blouses, long blonde hair and billowing kaftans which reflected a period of hippie chic at the beginning of the 1970s. The Coca-Cola advert of 1971, featuring the song 'I'd Like to Teach the World to Sing' sums up the fashions

Contrasting 1970s fashions including flares and a Starsky and Hutch influenced jumper.

Cut-off flared trousers were all the rage for a while, complete with bright wide-collared shirts, short denim jackets and Doc Martens.

of the early part of the decade where remnants of the 1960s were still in place. The song was a hit for the New Seekers the following year.

Platform shoes became very popular in the mid–1970s and the size of the platforms got larger and larger. Clog-style shoes were also very popular. The style was bolstered by the glam rock stars of the day who over-exaggerated the fashion.

Every week on Top of the Pops the fashions got wilder and wilder. Male pop stars such as Marc Bolan, Bryan Ferry and Roy Wood would appear, complete with make-up, in the latest trends, including animal print tops and suits, gold lurex trousers, glittery jackets (in garish colours), wild, dyed hair of various hues, silver waistcoats, feather boas and tartan, as well as colourful leather trousers and jackets.

Platform shoes also came in a variety of colours complete with stripes, stars, glitter and Union Jacks with heels, the bigger the better. Top hats were worn by stars such as Marc Bolan and Noddy Holder of Slade. Holder's hat, cleverly decorated with round mirrors, became his trademark.

Oxford bags made a comeback in the 1970s having previously been worn between the 1920s and 1950s. Trousers in the 1970s were loose fitting and often came in a range of checked fabrics including plaid and tartan. Male and female teenagers often wore cut-off or knee length versions complete with platform shoes or Doc Marten boots. Braces, large belts and short-cropped jackets completed the look.

Huge flares worn with platform shoes together with brightly patterned shirts with large wing collars were seen everywhere. Even people not into the latest fashions found it impossible to buy a pair of trousers or jeans that didn't have flares. For a while, week by week, flares seemed to increase in size as did shirt collar sizes and the heels on platform shoes. Denim shirts and flared jeans became the decade's casual wear and were worn by both men and women.

Fashions of the mid-1970s included flared trousers, wing collars, checked shirts and 'bovver boots'.

Boys wore green parka coats with orange linings and hoods lined with rabbit fur. T-shirts appeared covered in a variety of statements and slogans including iron-on transfers featuring jokes, tv stars and programmes, pop singers and iconic characters such as Che Guevara. Shops popped up everywhere ready to put whatever you wanted on a T-shirt. Music and television played a huge part in influencing fashions.

Fans gather at a Bay City Rollers concert. Girls can be seen wearing tartan together with wing-collared shirts, scarves and hats.

More Bay City Roller fans complete with flared cut-off trousers and tartan scarves and jackets.

The Hammersmith Odeon announcing the arrival of the Bay City Rollers.

With the Bay City Rollers at their height, girls dressed in tartan with cut-off short trousers, braces, scarves and short fitted jackets. When Starsky and Hutch appeared on television, everyone wanted a copy of Starsky's heavy large-patterned jumper. Knitting companies quickly issued patterns so that people could knit their own.

Rock and Roll played a major part in the charts during the 1970s with popular bands of the day being Mud, Darts and Showaddywaddy while Happy Days, complete with The Fonz, appeared on the television. Meanwhile, the movie *Grease* played at the cinema and created a revival in the rock and roll era of the 1950s. Fashions matched the trend with leather jackets, drainpipe trousers and crepe shoes. Although the Ramones were essentially described as punks, their clothing fitted a more rock and roll image.

In 1972 Diane von Furstenberg became a fashion icon when she created the wrap dress. In the following five years, it sold to millions and was seen as a symbol of 'female power' as women entered the

Two Bay City Rollers fans, in the latest fashions, waiting to see the band.

workplace on a larger scale. In 1997 it was relaunched and in 2005, von Furstenberg was presented with a Council of Fashion Designers of America Lifetime Achievement Award.

Laura Ashley introduced Edwardian-style dresses with romantic silhouettes and floral-covered prints during the 1970s which proved popular. Meanwhile, Yves Saint Laurent became known for creating trousers that were acceptable for women to wear to work. Before the 1970s women mainly only wore trousers at home. In 1966 Saint Laurent designed the city trouser and in 1968, introduced women's trouser suits including the safari suit. The fashion became popular in the 1970s and still continues to this day.

Biba, Barbara Hulanicki's London boutique, sold bell-bottom power suits for women in checked patterns or highly saturated colours. Mail order meant that women around the country could easily purchase the clothes.

Roy Halston Frowick created the jersey halter dress as well as minimalistic draped gowns. The legendary designer was better known as just 'Halston'. He also created knitwear, turtlenecks, sweaters,

Men of the decade dressed in the latest fashions. Plaid flared trousers were very popular, as were satin or checked shirts, large ties and two-tone shoes.

sweater sets, boxy square jackets and wide-legged jersey trousers. He was a social icon during the 1970s and was known for frequenting the cool clubs of New York such as Studio 54.

For a while men wore safari suits with cut-off sleeves. They came in a variety of colours but light tan seemed to be popular. It was never a good look and luckily didn't last very long, although it was far more popular in Australia where they were seen as acceptable business suits. Men who wore safari suits usually had longish hair, Jason King-type moustaches, and wore open shirts which revealed hairy chests with either a gold crucifix or St Christopher medallion around their neck.

In the later 1970s punk played a large part in fashion, for a minority, with ripped T-shirts and jeans featuring zips and safety pins, together with leather trousers and jackets. For a while, for a few, even bin bags

Punk fashions of the late 1970s. The fashion included torn T-shirts, leather trousers and jackets complete with spiked hair, smudged make-up, zips, chains and safety pins.

became fashionable. The fashion caught on with the influence of designers such as Vivienne Westwood and Malcolm McLaren who promoted the Sex Pistols. Other bands which adopted the fashion included Siouxsie and the Banshees, X-Ray Spex, the Damned and UK Subs. Vivienne Westwood began by making clothes for Malcolm McLaren's boutique in King's Road. The unique clothing and music shaped the punk scene which was largely dominated by McLaren's band, the Sex Pistols. She said at the time, 'I was messianic about punk, seeing if one could put a spoke in the system in some way.' The fashion included razor blades, safety pins, clothing decorated with bicycle or lavatory chains as well as spiked dog collars for jewellery, outrageous hair, often spiked, and eye-catching make-up. The Sex Pistols band members Johnny Rotten and Sid Vicious, as well as Siouxsie Sioux became, probably unintentionally, fashion icons and their image was copied by the young and dispossessed everywhere.

The Teddy Boy fashion was very popular with rockers in the 1970s. Bands such as Wizzard, Mud and Showaddywaddy bolstered the trend. The clothes were inspired by those worn by dandies in the Edwardian era. The look became popular in the 1950s during the rock and roll era and wearers were known as 'Cosher Boys'. The *Daily Express* renamed them 'Teddy Boys' in 1953, by shortening the word 'Edwardian' to 'Teddy' and the name stuck. The fashion included tapered trousers, fancy waistcoats and long jackets similar to the American zoot suits of the time. 'Brothel creeper' shoes and Tony Curtis hairstyles completed the look. In the 1970s the style was promoted by Vivienne Westwood and Malcolm McLaren in their shop Let it Rock, located on King's Road, London. The fashion was influenced by the glam rock era and featured louder colours complete with brightly coloured socks, satin shirts and bootlace ties. The revival of rockabilly music also led to exaggerations of the original DA hairstyles and featured large quiffs. Flamboyant pompadour hairstyles were accompanied by long sideburns. Punk grew out of this fashion although punks and teddy boys were great rivals and in the spring of 1977, street battles took place on London's King's Road between the two groups. Popular music and the death of Elvis Presley inspired the interest in rock and roll music and enhanced the rocker look even further. Punk took on elements of rockers such as Elvis. The cover of the Clash's first album took its styling directly from the cover of Presley's first album with its infamous pink and green lettering.

At the same time, the world was introduced to the movie, *Saturday Night Fever* and disco fashion took off with tight-fitting suits, platform shoes, black, white or brightly-coloured shirts with large collars for men and flowing dresses for women.

Hairstyles varied greatly over the 1970s with television playing a part in influencing some. When Farrah Fawcett appeared in Charlie's Angels in the mid–1970s with her long flicked hair, women world–wide followed suit. Perms became fashionable for both sexes. Male television stars suddenly appeared with permed hair including comedians Bobby

Ball, Eddie Large and Lennie Bennett. The style appeared to work better on women but, for a while, it also proved popular with men.

Other hairstyles that were popular for women in the 1970s included the Shag, which was invented by hairdresser Paul McGregor and was worn by Jane Fonda in *Klute*. In 1974, Trevor Sorbie, the British hair stylist created the Wedge with its short, layered, angular style.

Hair got longer in the early 1970s. Many men grew their hair over their ears, others grew sideburns and wild Burt Reynolds–type moustaches. Suddenly, there were more hair products for men. In the past hairspray had been just for women but now there were brands for men including, the most remembered, Cossack. Many schoolboys began to have long and shaggy hairstyles. With the glam rock bands came the feather cut which was popular for the period and can be seen worn by members of bands such as the Sweet, Slade, Roxy Music and artists such as David Bowie, Rod Stewart and Suzi Quatro.

Afro haircuts were very popular for black Americans in the early 1970s and the style is reflected in movies such as *Shaft* as well as in bands of the day including the Stylistics and the Jacksons. Teddy Boys and Rockers wore their hair in a DA style kept in place with the use of products such as Brylcreem. Later, Punks had cropped hair, shaved heads or magnificent sculptured styles such as horns and spikes or the infamous Mohican, which came in a range of colors.

In 1976 a new hairstyle appeared on the scene when Joanna Lumley appeared in The New Avengers. She played Purdey and wore her hair in a bowl-shape pageboy style. The cut was soon sought after by women in the UK and the style became known as the Purdey. Flicks and wings were popular with girls and had been around long before Farrah Fawcett appeared in Charlie's Angels in 1976. The style was created by using rollers and tongs combined with perms.

When Bo Derek ran along the beach in the film *10* in 1979, suddenly every women wanted to copy her braided hair and, again, a movie had influenced fashion.

Bands such as the Jam promoted the Mod image towards the end of the 1970s with smart, well-fitting suits and pencil-thin ties.

The Ska fashion had been popular in the 1960s but resurfaced in the late 1970s as part of 2 Tone music. Bands that promoted the image included Madness, the Specials, the Beat, the Selecter and Bad Manners. The fashion was much admired by skinheads. Fans of the music were known as Rude boys and Rude girls named after Jamaican street gangsters who were known for their stylish way of dressing. The style borrowed from other trends including skinhead, punk and Teddy Boys. Shoes worn included loafers, Doc Martens or Gibsons or brogues, while girls wore monkey boots or winkle pickers complete with heels. Harrington jackets with tartan linings were worn together with v-neck jumpers as well as check patterned or block coloured button-down Ben Sherman shirts. Trousers were straight-legged jeans or well fitting cotton trousers. A pair of dark wraparound sunglasses (or Blues Brothers-type

Mods on scooters preparing for a day out complete with the fashions of the day. Classic mod scooters were manufactured by Vespa and Lambretta.

Wayfarers) together with a pork-pie hat or a trilby completed the look. Haircuts for men were short and included a flat top while girls wore their hair in a 1960s bob as well as in other styles.

The Mod revival of the late 1970s took the energy of punk mixed with the sound of 1960s music from bands such as the Who, Small Faces and the Kinks. The Jam was largely responsible for the revival and the movie *Quadrophenia* (1979) added to the trend. Mods wore smart clothes including tailor-made suits with narrow lapels (some were made of mohair) and white, pin-striped or polo shirts. Accessories included thin ties and button-down collar shirts together with wool or cashmere jumpers, either crewneck or V-neck. Footwear included pointed shoes, Clarks desert boots, Chelsea or Beatle boots, loafers and bowling shoes. Fishtail parkas completed the look and became the symbol of the mod fashion. Baracuta Harrington jackets and Duffel coats were also worn.

The fashion was inspired by the beatniks and their bohemian style of black turtlenecks and berets as well as from the Teddy Boys smart, eye-catching, dandy look. Their hairstyles were neat and short and were originally inspired by French film stars such as Jean-Paul Belmondo and Alain Delon. The word 'mod' came from the word 'modernist' used to describe modern jazz musicians and their fans in the 1950s. In the 1960s Mods had notoriously fought with Rockers at seaside holiday resorts and the fights continued in the 1970s with skinheads fighting with Teddy Boys and rockers. In 1977, punks famously fought with Teddy Boys at Margate as well as at Brighton, Southend, Clacton, Hastings and Scarborough.

The skinhead fashion had been prevalent throughout the 1970s with members wearing tight jeans, Bovver Boots (Doc Martens), tight T-shirts, braces and bomber jackets. Skinheads were often linked to racism and violence but many were just driven by the music and culture of the time.

The decade ended with several fashions including punk, rock and Mod. The 1970s had certainly seen some outrageous fashions, many of which have been repeated ever since but not to such a wild degree as in the glam and punk rock periods, although elements of the fashions are still with us today.

Celebrity quotes:

'Fashion is not something that exists in dresses only. Fashion is in the sky, in the street, fashion has to do with ideas, the way we live, what is happening.' Coco Chanel.

'Fashion is mysterious, as a rule. Why are blue jeans a classic? You just hit on something that happens to be timeless and right.' Diane von Furstenberg.

'If you wear clothes that don't suit you, you're a fashion victim. You have to wear clothes that make you look better.' Vivienne Westwood.

'I always said punk was an attitude. It was never about having a Mohican haircut or wearing a ripped T-shirt. It was all about destruction and the creative potential within that.' Malcolm McLaren.

'My entire life, socially, was all around the Maggie era. That was the great challenge as a Sex Pistol was how to deal with Margaret Thatcher. I think we did rather good.' John Lydon (Johnny Rotten).

'It is almost better to be an impulse shirt-buyer than an impulse shoe-buyer. I have worn shirts that made people think I was a retired Mafia hit-man or a Yugoslavian sports convener from Split, but I have worn shoes that made people think I was insane.' Clive James.

Chapter 3

Music

The 1970s opened with acts such as Edison Lighthouse 'Love Grows' ('Where My Rosemary Goes'), Lee Marvin ('Wandrin Star'), Simon and Garfunkel ('Bridge Over Troubled Water'), Dana ('All Kinds of Everything') and Christie ('Yellow River'). Dana topped the charts after winning the Eurovision Song Contest. Norman Greenbaum reached number one in March 1970 with 'Spirit in the Sky' and went on to sell two million copies.

Some of the best acts of 1970 didn't reach the top position in the charts such as 'I Want You Back' by the Jacksons (number two), 'Instant Karma!' by John Lennon, Yoko Ono and the Plastic Ono Band (number five), 'Let It Be' by The Beatles (number two), 'Young Gifted And Black' by Bob and Marcia and 'Never Had A Dream Come True' by Stevie Wonder (number six).

England had high hopes of winning the World Cup in 1970 and the team recorded 'Back Home' which went straight to number one. Unfortunately, the team didn't do so well in Mexico and were defeated in the quarter-final.

As the decade moved on, a whole new wave of music entered the charts as well as a few old favourites. The music of the 1970s included all kinds of genres including middle of the road, glam, country, rock and roll, punk (new wave), mod, disco, heavy metal and everything in between.

Glam rock introduced groups such as Wizzard, Slade, Mud, T-Rex, Roxy Music, the Sweet and Queen with more poppy bands such as the Rubettes, Kenny, Sailor and Showaddywaddy, The Bay City Rollers and Slik.

Noddy Holder, of Slade, performing on stage with the band, together with guitar, purple shirt and mirrored top hat.

Singers from the glam rock era included David Bowie, Elton John, Bryan Ferry, Marc Bolan, Freddie Mercury as well as Suzi Quatro, David Essex and Alvin Stardust.

Glam Rock took off in 1971 and Marc Bolan's appearance on Top of the Pops in March of that year, dressed in glitter and satins, singing his hit 'Hot Love' was said to have kicked it all off. By late 1971 David Bowie had developed the character Ziggy Stardust and incorporated makeup, mime, wild fashion and performance into his act. Soon, other acts such as Roxy Music, Sweet, Slade, Mott the Hoople and Alvin Stardust were following suit.

Queen's Freddie Mercury performing live on stage.

David Bowie performing on stage during the 1970s. His hits during the decade included 'Starman' (1972), 'The Jean Genie' (1972), 'Life on Mars' (1973), 'Rebel, Rebel' (1974), 'Space Oddity' (1975) and 'Heroes' (1977) as well as many others.

Dave Hill, Slade's most glam member, complete with make-up, glitter and medallion.

Roxy Music's glammed-up lead singer, Bryan Ferry dressed in a sequined jacket. Fondly remembered for 1970s hits, 'Virginia Plain', 'Do the Strand' and 'Love is the Drug'.

A second wave of glam rock included artists such as Suzi Quatro, Wizzard and Sparks and their music dominated the charts between 1974 and 1976. Elton John, Queen and Rod Stewart also adopted the glam style. Wild, ostentatious clothes added to the fashion of the period and included platform shoes, flared trousers and large wing-collared shirts. The clothes that were worn by normal people were highly exaggerated by the pop performers of the day.

Side by side with the Glam rock hits of 1971 were unexpected number ones such as 'Grandad' by Clive Dunn, 'Knock Three Times' by Tony Orlando and Dawn, 'Chirpy Chirpy Cheep Cheep' by Middle of the Road and 'Ernie' by Benny Hill. In fact the only glam rock songs to reach number one during the year were 'Coz I Luv You' by Slade and T-Rex's two hits, 'Get It On' and 'Hot Love'.

Other top ten artists of 1971 included George Harrison ('My Sweet Lord'), The Tams ('Hey Girl Don't Bother Me'), Diana Ross ('I'm Still Waiting'), Nancy Sinatra and Lee Hazlewood ('Did You Ever') and Tony Christie ('I Did What I Did For Maria').

Slade performing on stage. Noddy Holder is wearing tartan trousers and braces as well as his trademark mirrored top hat.

The year 1972 saw further glam number ones with 'Telegram Sam' and 'Metal Guru' both from T-Rex. Slade had hits with 'Take Me Bak 'Ome' and 'Mama Weer All Crazee Now'. Other hits of the year came from the New Seekers ('I'd Like to Teach the World to Sing'), Chickory Tip ('Son of My Father'), Nilsson ('Without You'), The Royal Scots Dragoon Guards ('Amazing Grace'), Don McLean ('Vincent'), Alice Cooper ('School's Out'), Rod Stewart ('You Wear It Well'), Lieutenant Pigeon ('Mouldy Old Dough'), Gilbert O'Sullivan ('Clair') and Chuck Berry ('My Ding-a-Ling'). This was a novelty song and was Chuck Berry's only UK number one. British morality campaigner, Mary Whitehouse, objected to the lyrics and called for the song to be banned. The other surprise hit of the year came from Lieutenant Pigeon with 'Mouldy Old Dough'. The band was fronted by Rob Woodward and his 60-year-old mother, Hilda, played the piano. It seemed an unlikely combination for Top of the Pops but the song was soon a hit. Other members of the band included drummer Nigel Fletcher and bassist Stephen Johnson.

'Clair' was Gilbert O'Sullivan's first number one but he had previously had hits with 'Nothing Rhymed', 'No Matter How I Try', 'Alone Again (Naturally)' and 'Ooh-Wakka-Doo-Wakka-Day'. He appeared on Top of the Pops and other music programmes wearing a cloth cap over a basin haircut, grey jacket and waistcoat and schoolboy shorts. It was an odd look, even at the time, but soon got him noticed.

In the summer of 1972, Donny Osmond topped the UK charts with 'Puppy Love'. Screaming girls met the 14-year-old sensation wherever he went and caused havoc at airports. Osmondmania soon took off and it wasn't long before the rest of the family were joining in. By November 1972 the Osmonds (Donny, Merrill, Alan, Jay and Wayne) had reached number two in the UK singles chart with 'Crazy Horses'. In December 1972, Donny's brother, the 9-year-old 'Little Jimmy Osmond' had a number one hit with 'Long Haired Lover from Liverpool'. The song remained at the top spot for five weeks and sold over a million copies. Like the Jacksons before them, the Osmonds also had their own cartoon series. Marie Osmond, just 13 years old, hit the charts the following year with 'Paper Roses'. In 1974 the Osmonds hit number one in the UK with 'Love Me For a Reason'. By that time, both Donny and Marie had their own show in the US which was also broadcast in the UK.

During 1972 David Cassidy was every bit as popular as Donny Osmond and his brothers. He was already the star of the Partridge Family, first broadcast in 1970. He hit the charts in 1972 in the UK with 'Could It Be Forever/Cherish' which went to number two in April and 'How Can I Be Sure' which went to number one in September. Further hits followed and he hit the number one spot again in October 1973 with 'Daydreamer'. He continued to have top twenty hits throughout 1975.

Number one records of 1973 included many Glam rock hits. These included 'Blockbuster' by Sweet, 'Cum on Feel the Noize' by Slade, 'See My Baby Jive' by Wizzard, 'Can the Can' by Suzi Quatro, 'Skweeze Me Pleeze Me' again by Slade, 'I'm the Leader of the Gang'

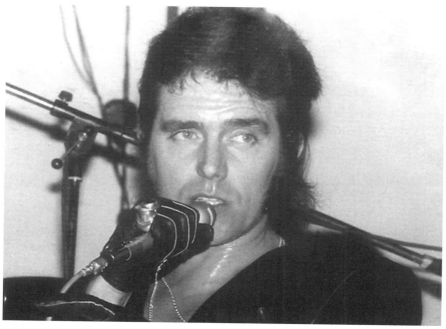

Alvin Stardust complete with quiffed hair and fake sideburns. His hits included 'My Coo Ca Choo', 'Jealous Mind' and 'You, You, You'.

by Gary Glitter, 'Angel Fingers' by Wizzard and 'I Love You Love Me Love' by Gary Glitter. The number one glam Christmas record was 'Merry Xmas Everybody' by Slade, which has been played every Christmas since.

Other number ones of 1973 included 'The Twelfth of Never' by Donny Osmond, 'Get Down' by Gilbert O'Sullivan, 'Tie a Yellow Ribbon Round the Ole Oak Tree' by Dawn featuring Tony Orlando, 'Rubber Bullets' by 10cc, 'Welcome Home' by Peters and Lee, 'Young Love' by Donny Osmond, 'Eye Level' (the theme from Van Der Valk) by the Simon Park Orchestra and, as mentioned earlier, 'Daydreamer' by David Cassidy.

Peters and Lee proved hugely popular after winning the talent show Opportunity Knocks seven times. Their record 'Welcome Home' went on to sell 800,000 copies. They appeared as guests on many television shows and also had their own show, Meet Peters and Lee.

Suzi Quatro complete with leather jumpsuit. Her hits in the 1970s included 'Can the Can' and 'Devil Gate Drive'.

'Tie a Yellow Ribbon Round the Ole Oak Tree' was a huge hit by Dawn featuring Tony Orlando and stayed at number one for four weeks. The record went on to sell over three million copies.

Glam rock again featured heavily in 1974 with the number ones being 'Tiger Feet' by Mud, 'Devil Gate Drive' by Suzi Quatro, 'Jealous Mind' by Alvin Stardust, 'Sugar Baby Love' by the Rubettes, 'Gonna Make You a Star' by David Essex and 'Always Yours' by Gary Glitter. Other hits of the year included 'You Won't Find Another Fool Like Me' by the New Seekers, 'Billy Don't Be a Hero' by Paper Lace, 'Seasons in the Sun' by Terry Jacks, 'The Streak' by Ray Stevens, 'She' by Charles Aznavour, 'Rock Your Baby' by George McCrae, 'When Will I See You Again' by the Three Degrees, 'Love Me For a Reason' by the Osmonds, 'Kung Fu Fighting' by Karl Douglas, 'Annie's Song' by John Denver, 'Sad Sweet Dreamer' by Sweet Sensation, 'Everything I Own' by Ken Boothe and 'You're the First, the Last, My Everything' by Barry White.

ABBA went to the top spot in May with their first hit of many, 'Waterloo', after winning the Eurovision Song Contest. The year ended with the Christmas number one, 'Lonely This Christmas' by Mud, again played every year since.

Amazingly, the most successful act of 1974 was the Wombles. Their three hits during that year were 'Minuetto Allegretto', 'Remember You're A Womble' and 'Wombling Merry Christmas'. None of their songs went to number one in the charts but their albums remained in the charts for many weeks during 1974. 'Wombling Merry Christmas' went to number two and was just kept off the top spot by Mud. More hits followed in 1975 and, for a while, the Wombles were part of the glam scene.

The Goodies were another novelty band who had hits between 1974 and 1975 although none reached number one. Their record 'The Inbetweenies' reached number seven in 1974 and 'Funky Gibbon' reached number four in the following year.

'Kung Fu Fighting' by Karl Douglas hit the charts after the incredible success of the tv series Kung Fu starring David Carradine and the many Kung Fu movies, such as *Enter the Dragon*, starring Bruce Lee.

By 1975 Rollermania was sweeping the country. The Bay City Rollers had had their first hit in 1971 with 'Keep On Dancing' which reached number nine in the UK chart. They failed to chart in 1972 but were back in 1973 with 'Remember (Sha La La La)', 'Shang-A-Lang', 'Summerlove Sensation' and 'All of Me Loves All of You'.

By 1975 they scored their first number one hit with 'Bye, Bye, Baby' and 'Give A Little Love'. The band consisted of Les McKeown, Alan Longmuir, Derek Longmuir, Stuart 'Woody' Wood and Eric Faulkner. Their popularity exploded after the success of 'Remember' and by 1975 they became one of the highest selling acts in the UK. Their popularity was compared to that of the Beatles and screaming girls, dressed in appropriate Roller fashions, followed them everywhere. This led to the Rollers being given their own 20-week tv series called Shang-A-Lang. 'Bye, Bye, Baby', a cover of the Four Seasons song, stayed at number one for six weeks and sold nearly a million copies. In late 1975, the Rollers reached number one on the US Billboard chart with 'Saturday Night' and their album 'Bay City Rollers' (which was only released in North America) hit the number one spot in February

Rod Stewart and members of the Faces backstage. Number Ones of the decade for Stewart included 'Maggie May', 'You Wear It Well', 'Sailing', 'I Don't Want to Talk About It' / 'The First Cut is the Deepest' and 'Da Ya Think I'm Sexy'.

of that year. The band were also hugely popular in Australia where they were met by thousands of screaming fans, complete in cut-off tartan trousers and scarves. By early 1976, because of the strain of success, Alan Longmuir decided to leave the group and was replaced by Ian Mitchell. The band had further hits including 'Dedication' and 'I Only Want to Be With You'. By 1977 their popularity had waned and there were several replacement band members but they never again achieved their earlier success.

Kojak was very popular in 1975 and Telly Savalas scored a number one hit that year with 'If' which mainly featured him speaking the lyrics. As mentioned, the Bay City Rollers had two number one hits in 1975.

Other number ones included 'Down Down' by Status Quo, 'Ms Grace' by the Tymes, 'January' by Pilot, 'Make Me Smile' by Steve Harley and Cockney Rebel, 'Oh Boy' by Mud, 'Stand By Your Man' by Tammy Wynette, 'I'm Not in Love' by 10cc, 'Tears on My Pillow' by Johnny Nash, 'Barbados' by Typically Tropical, 'Can't Give You Anything But My Love' by the Stylistics, 'Sailing' by Rod Stewart, 'Hold Me Close' by David Essex, 'I Only Have Eyes For You' by Art Garfunkel and 'D.I.V.O.R.C.E.' by Billy Connolly which was a send up of the Tammy Wynette song. The huge hits of the year were 'Space Oddity' by David Bowie and 'Bohemian Rhapsody' by Queen, which stayed at the top of the chart for nine weeks.

The punk look of the later 1970s. A Sex Pistols 'God Save the Queen' Union Jack can be seen in the background.

By 1976, Glam was on its way out. Many bands of the day continued to perform, but punk rock was now entering the charts. Bands such as the Sex Pistols shocked the nation with their apparent wild acts of debauchery and were soon followed by others such as the Clash, the Damned, Siouxsie and the Banshees, the Buzzcocks, the Stranglers, X-Ray Spex, the Adverts and UK Subs.

Fashion, again, played a huge part in the music and included Vivienne Westwood designs with torn clothes, zips, safety pins, offensive T-shirts, leather jackets, kilts, bin liners with spiked piercings, razor blades as jewellery, complete with military boots, brothel creepers or Dr Martens. Punk hairstyles included short spiked hair as well as Mohican haircuts. There were no punk tunes as number ones in 1976, however.

ABBA hit the number one spot three times with 'Mamma Mia', 'Fernando' and 'Dancing Queen'. The only disco hit was 'I Love to Love' from Tina Charles. Other number ones came from Slik ('Forever

Hugh Cornwell playing with The Stranglers. Their hits in the 1970s included 'Peaches', 'Something Better Change', and 'No More Heroes'.

Siouxsie Sioux, of
Siouxsie and the Banshees,
whose biggest hit was
'Hong Kong Garden' in
1978.

and Ever'), the Four Seasons ('December 1963'), Brotherhood of Man
('Save Your Kisses for Me'), J.J. Barrie ('No Charge'), the Wurzels
('The Combine Harvester'), Real Thing ('You to Me Are Everything'),
Demis Roussos ('Forever and Ever'), Elton John and Kiki Dee ('Don't
Go Breaking My Heart'), Pussycat ('Mississippi'), Chicago ('If You
Leave Me Now') and Showaddywaddy ('Under the Moon of Love').
The Christmas number one was 'When A Child is Born' by Johnny
Mathis.

Amazingly, although the Sex Pistols were dominating the news,
'Anarchy' in the UK only reached number thirty-eight.

By 1977, with the popularity of the US television series Starsky and
Hutch, David Soul had his first number one in January with 'Don't Give
Up On Us' which stayed at the top spot for four weeks. This was followed
by 'Don't Cry For Me, Argentina' by Julie Covington, which came from
the stage musical, *Evita*. Disco hits to hit the top spot in 1977 included

'I Feel Love' by Donna Summer (which was played everywhere that year) and 'Yes Sir, I Can Boogie' by Baccara. ABBA had two more number one hits that year which included 'Knowing Me, Knowing You' and 'The Name of the Game'. Other number ones came from Leo Sayer ('When I Need You'), the Manhatten Transfer ('Chanson d'Amour'), Deniece Williams ('Free'), Rod Stewart ('I Don't Want To Talk About It'/' The First Cut is the Deepest'), Kenny Rogers ('Lucille'), the Jacksons ('Show You the Way to Go'), Hot Chocolate ('So You Win Again'), Brotherhood of Man ('Angelo') and the Floaters ('Float On').

With the death of Elvis Presley in 1977, Rock and Roll once more became fashionable, although it had never really gone away. On the evening of 16 August news reached the UK of Elvis's death via Reginald Bosanquet and the ITN news. Radio stations all around the world played continuous Elvis records and newspapers and television news carried little else. Suddenly, Elvis Presley records were again selling in great numbers. Never again since has the death of a music star been reported so widely and for so long.

The notorious punk band the Sex Pistols performing live on stage. Many radio stations refused to play their hit, 'God Save the Queen' in 1977.

On 3 September Elvis reached number one with 'Way Down' and stayed there for five weeks. Elvis fans were annoyed when David Soul knocked him off the top spot with 'Silver Lady'. The Christmas number one was 'Mull of Kintyre' by Wings.

Meanwhile, disco hit the charts with the release of the film *Saturday Night Fever* featuring a soundtrack by the Bee Gees.

The Sex Pistols had their highest chart entry with 'God Save the Queen' which went to number two in 1977. 'Pretty Vacant' reached number six soon after. 'God Save the Queen' was released during the Silver Jubilee but the BBC refused to play the song. Subsequently, it went to number one in the *New Musical Express* (NME) chart. It was believed to have been the biggest selling single at the time even though it was kept off the top of the official chart because it was feared that it might offend. Rod Stewart appeared in the number one spot whilst the number two spot on Top of the Pops was just left blank. Both the BBC and the Independent Broadcasting Authority banned the song.

Bill posters advertising the latest bands including Motorhead, Sad Cafe and Squeeze.

The first number one of 1978 was 'Uptown Top Ranking' by Althea and Donna which was followed by Brotherhood of Man's hit, 'Figaro'. In February, ABBA again reached the number one spot with 'Take a Chance on Me'.

The most unusual and different hit of the year came from Kate Bush with her first release 'Wuthering Heights'. Her appearance on Top of the Pops had everyone talking about her the next day. In April Brian and Michael scored a hit with the novelty song 'Matchstalk Men and Matchstalk Cats and Dogs' (about the painter L.S. Lowry) which stayed at number one for three weeks.

The success in the cinema of *Saturday Night Fever* saw the Bee Gees at number one for two weeks during April and May. Another hit movie featuring John Travolta, *Grease*, saw many chart hits from the film with the two number ones during 1978 being 'You're the One That I Want' and 'Summer Nights', both featuring John Travolta and Olivia Newton-John. Other number ones of 1978 included 'Rivers of Babylon' by Boney M, 'Three Times a Lady' by the Commodores,

Elvis Costello performing during the punk days. Chart hits included 'Watching the Detectives', 'Alison', 'Pump It Up' and 'Oliver's Army'.

'Dreadlock Holiday' by 10cc, 'Rat Trap' by the Boomtown Rats and 'Da Ya Think I'm Sexy' by Rod Stewart. The Christmas number one was 'Mary's Boy Child' by Boney M.

In 1979, 2 Tone emerged with bands such as Madness and the Specials while electropop hit the charts with Gary Numan and Tubeway Army. The UK's first rap song also hit the charts that year and came from the Sugar Hill Gang ('Rapper's Delight'). Blondie, The Bee Gees, The Police, Ian Dury and the Blockheads, the Boomtown Rats, Elvis Costello and the Village People all appeared in the charts that year. More middle of the road songs came from Lena Martell ('One Day At A Time'), Art Garfunkel ('Bright Eyes') and Dr Hook ('When You're In Love With A Beautiful Woman'). The best selling album of the year was 'Parallel Lines' from Blondie.

The first number one came from the Village People with 'YMCA'. The song stayed at the top of the charts for three weeks before being

A studio shot of Blondie featuring Debbie Harry, Gary Valentine, Clem Burke, Chris Stein and Jimmy Destri. The band featured in the charts many times in the late 1970s with hits such as 'Denis', 'Picture This', 'Hanging on the Telephone', 'Heart of Glass' and 'Sunday Girl'.

replaced with 'Hit Me With Your Rhythm Stick' by Ian Dury and the Blockheads. Blondie scored two number one hits during the year which were 'Heart of Glass' and 'Sunday Girl'. The Bee Gees hit the top spot again with a song from *Saturday Night Fever*, 'Tragedy'. Gary Numan had two hits during 1979, the first with Tubeway Army being 'Are Friends Electric' and the second as himself with 'Cars'. Art Garfunkel topped the charts for six weeks with 'Bright Eyes' which came from the film *Watership Down*. Other number ones of the year were 'I Will Survive' by Gloria Gaynor, 'Ring My Bell' by Anita Ward, 'I Don't Like Mondays' by the Boomtown Rats, 'We Don't Talk Anymore' by Cliff Richard, 'Message in a Bottle' by The Police, 'Video Killed the Radio Star' by the Buggles, 'One Day at a Time' by Lena Martell, 'When You're in Love with a Beautiful Woman' by Dr Hook and 'Walking on the Moon' by The Police. The Christmas number one and the last number one of the 1970s was 'Another Brick in the Wall' by Pink Floyd, which stayed at the top of the charts for five weeks.

Celebrity quotes:

'*I don't know where I'm going from here, but I promise it won't be boring.*' David Bowie.

'*There is so little time for us all; I need to be able to say what I want quickly and to as many people as possible.*' Marc Bolan.

'*I've had a great metamorphosis in my life. I struggled for a number of years because I was identified with that image of the Seventies.*' David Cassidy.

'*I'm not here for your amusement. You're here for mine.*' Johnny Rotten, The Sex Pistols.

'*I never intended for the Sex Pistols to be immeasurably successful.*' Malcolm McLaren.

'*Business opportunities are like buses, there's always another one coming.*' Richard Branson.

Chapter 4

Television

By the early 1970s most homes had a television set. They were usually hired from a local electrical outlet such as Rumbelows or DER. TVs had three channels including BBC1, BBC2 and ITV, which also included regional programmes. Television stations closed down around midnight after playing the National Anthem. There were no remote controls and channels on televisions had to be changed manually. The more modern sets had push buttons to change channels but most had a dial which had to be tuned in to get the best signal. Table-top aerials were popular which plugged into the back of the tv and had to be adjusted to get a strong signal. Even pointing it in the direction of the nearest transmitter usually resulted in much ghosting and the picture was quite often poor, especially in bad weather conditions.

All televisions at the beginning of the 1970s were black and white sets, even though the television companies had started broadcasting in colour. It was easy to see which programmes were in colour because the presenters, including the men, were heavily made-up.

Whole families gathered around the one household television to watch dramas, comedies, music shows and films although many of the films seemed to date from the 1950s and before. Children's television would be broadcast before 6pm with the ever-popular Magic Roundabout being shown just before the news.

The television sets were bulky although very modern at the time. Owning your own television was almost unheard of for ordinary families. In 1974 colour televisions started to appear. Some well-off families had them before but suddenly there was a high demand for the new sets. Many people still rented but, for the first time, some bought their own sets. They weren't cheap and retailed at about £420 for a set with a 20-inch screen. Even with their high price, there were still no remote controls and arguments would break out over who was going to 'turn the telly over'.

The decade started well with many wonderful programmes. Popular television shows in 1970 included the talent show Opportunity Knocks and police dramas such as Z Cars and Dixon of Dock Green.

Jon Pertwee became the new Doctor Who in January 1970 much to the dismay of many children who had grown accustomed to watching Patrick Troughton in the role. He made his first appearance in the show on 3 January in 'Spearhead in Space' which was the first Doctor Who serial to be broadcast in colour. Pertwee made the role his own and gathered a new collection of fans who soon forgot Troughton. By 1974 Tom Baker took over the role of the Doctor complete with floppy hat and long scarf. He remained in the show longer than any other actor and became hugely popular in the part which saw him fighting both the Daleks and the Cybermen with his long-term assistants Sarah Jane Smith (Elisabeth Sladen), Harry Sullivan (Ian Marter) and his robotic dog, K-9. He was later assisted by Leela (Louise Jameson) and Romana (played by both Mary Tamm and Lalla Ward). He was eventually replaced by Peter Davison in 1981.

The Six Wives of Henry VIII, starring Keith Michell, was broadcast in January 1970 and was greatly enjoyed by adult audiences. The six-part series was eventually made into a film, again with Keith Michell in the lead role.

In November of the same year, there was a colour strike when staff at ITV refused to use the new colour equipment because of a dispute over pay. It made little difference to most viewers who were all watching in black and white anyway.

On BBC1, new shows included A Question of Sport, Doomwatch, The Nine O'Clock News, Bachelor Father and Play for Today. For the children, there was Words and Pictures and the fondly remembered Mr Benn.

On BBC2 in November, The Goodies was first broadcast starring Tim Brooke-Taylor, Graeme Garden and Bill Oddie. The show ran until 1982.

World of Sport's main presenter throughout the 1970s, Dickie Davies. The show featured football, horse racing, wrestling and a range of unusual items such as Evel Knievel's leap over thirteen London buses. The show ran from 1965 until 1985.

Shows which had been broadcast for many years previously continued to be aired including Steptoe and Son (1962-74), Come Dancing (1949-98), The Good Old Days (1953-83), This Week (1956-92), Armchair Theatre (1956-74), The Sky at Night (1957-present) and, for sports fans, Grandstand (1958-2007), Match of the Day (1964-present) and World of Sport (1965-85).

ITV's popular shows in 1970 included Manhunt, A Family at War, Albert and Victoria, The Lovers and Queenie's Castle. For the children, new dramas included Timeslip and Gerry Anderson's UFO. Soaps included Coronation Street (1960-present) and Crossroads (1964-2003), complete with Noele Gordon and wobbly sets.

For teenagers, the most popular programme of the decade was Top of the Pops (1964-2006) which showcased the latest bands performing music from the Top 40.

Comedies included Please Sir! (1968-72), Father, Dear Father (1968-73), Dad's Army (1968-77), On the Buses (1969-73), Monty Python's Flying Circus (1969-74) and Never Mind the Quality, Feel the Width (1967-71). Other comedies of their time included Mind Your Language, Love Thy Neighbour and Till Death Us Do Part. Although acceptable in the 1970s, they are now seen as racist and bigoted and

One of Britain's best-loved comedians, Benny Hill. In 1971, he had a number one hit with 'Ernie (The Fastest Milkman in the West)'.

are never repeated unless shown on compilation programmes, which shows how times have changed.

Later much-loved programmes included And Mother Makes Three (1971-1973) starring Wendy Craig, Man About the House (1973-1976) starring Richard O'Sullivan, Paula Wilcox and Sally Thomsett, Porridge (1974-1977) starring the wonderful Ronnie Barker, Bless This House (1976) with Sid James and Diana Coupland, Butterflies (1978-1983), again starring Wendy Craig.

Some Mothers Do 'Ave 'Em (1973-1978) was an unmissable comedy for many and starred Michael Crawford as the hapless Frank Spencer and Michelle Dotrice as his doting wife, Betty. Many of the stunts featured in the programme were extremely dangerous and all were performed by Crawford himself. Catchphrases such as 'Ooh, Betty' and 'My cat's done a whoopsie' were copied by every school kid up and down the land as well as by the many impressionists on the television at the time.

Benny Hill was incredibly well-loved and his shows were watched by millions. His record, 'Ernie (The Fastest Milkman in the West)' topped the UK singles chart in 1971. The Benny Hill Show is still shown all over the world apart from in the UK where it is, perhaps unfairly, considered racist and sexist.

Other popular comedians of the 1970s who had their own shows included Les Dawson, Tommy Cooper, Frankie Howerd, Morecambe and Wise, The Two Ronnies and Harry Worth. The show The Comedians introduced a wealth of talent to television audiences including Mike Reid (later Frank Butcher in Eastenders), Frank Carson, Charlie Williams (a later host of The Golden Shot), Russ Abbot, Jim Bowen, Ken Goodwin, Bernard Manning, Tom O'Connor, Roy Walker and a host of other household names. The show ran from 1971 until 1974. A similar series, Who Do You Do, ran from 1972 until 1976 and introduced a variety of artists performing celebrity impressions. Stars who appeared on the show included Peter Goodwright, Janet Brown, Roger Kitter, Paul Melba, Johnnie More, Eddie Large, Syd Little, Russ Abbot, Les Dennis and Dustin Gee. It was hugely successful.

Budgie (1971) starred 1960s pop star Adam Faith as Ronald 'Budgie' Bird, a small time crook who had just been released from prison. The series followed his petty crimes aided and abetted by Charles Rendell (Iain Cuthbertson), a Glaswegian gangster who occasionally employed the hapless Budgie. There were two series of the show, each of thirteen episodes, and it proved very popular. A third series was planned but Faith was involved in a car crash and announced his retirement from acting. A spin-off series, Charles Endell Esquire, was released in 1979 but wasn't as successful partially due to a technicians strike which took it off air for three months.

The Onedin Line ran from 1971 to 1980. It was set in Liverpool starting in 1860 and revolved around a shipping owner, James Onedin, played by Peter Gilmore and his ongoing struggles with the business and his family. Memorable characters included Captain William Baines (Howard Lang), Anne Webster/Onedin (Anne Stallybrass), Elizabeth Onedin/Frazer/Fogarty (Jessica Benton) and Daniel Fogarty (Michael Billington). The show became unmissable Sunday night entertainment and featured memorable theme music, the Adagio from *Spartacus* by Khachaturian. Many of the outdoor scenes were filmed in the picturesque town of Dartmouth in Devon.

Gameshows included The Generation Game (with Bruce Forsyth), The Golden Shot (1967-75), It's a Knockout (1966-2001) and

Hughie Green presenter of the hugely successful talent show, Opportunity Knocks. Stars who found success on the show included Les Dawson, Peters and Lee and Lena Zavaroni.

Hughie Green on stage recording Thames Television's Opportunity Knocks.

Mr and Mrs (1964-99). The Generation Game was unmissable Saturday night entertainment and is well remembered for the prizes on the conveyer belt at the end including such exotic gifts as teasmades and carriage clocks. Bruce Forsyth hosted the show between 1971 and 1977. Larry Grayson, who took over in 1978, kept much of the show's appeal and stayed as presenter until 1981.

ITV had the Golden Shot (1967-75) where contestants in the studio and at home did their best to guide 'Bernie the Bolt' and his crossbow to shoot a dart through the centre of an apple. Breaking a string with the dart at the end of the show produced a shower of golden coins. Hosts in the 1970s included Bob Monkhouse, Norman Vaughan and Charlie Williams.

Sale of the Century ran from 1971 until 1983 and was hosted by Nicholas Parsons. It was described as the 'quiz of the week' and people tuned in to watch three contestants answer questions to compete for a range of prizes. The show was made originally just to be shown on Anglia Television but it gained nationwide coverage and became one of the most popular programmes on television.

Other quizshows of the 1970s included Celebrity Squares (1975-79), again with Bob Monkhouse, Name That Tune (1976) hosted by Tom O'Connor, Winner Takes All (1975-86) and 3-2-1 (1978-88) with Ted Rogers. There were many more.

Opportunity Knocks, hosted by Hughie Green, was an immensely popular talent show which ran until 1978. It was revived by the BBC in 1987 but never quite captured its original appeal. Stars made famous by the show in the 1970s included Su Pollard, Paul Daniels, Bobby Crush, Bonnie Langford, Little and Large, Peters and Lee, Lena Zavaroni, Frank Carson, Max Boyce, Pam Ayres and Les Dawson. Viewers voted for their favourite acts by post, but in the studio, acts were judged by the clapometer which rated the act on the volume of audience applause. Acts were weird and wonderful but always entertaining.

ITV had another popular talent show, New Faces, which ran between 1973 and 1978 and was hosted by Derek Hobson. Acts were judged by a panel of experts which included Tony Hatch, Mickie

Most, Clifford Davis, Arthur Askey, Ted Ray and others. Those made famous by the show included Lenny Henry, Les Dennis, Jim Davidson, Michael Barrymore, Victoria Wood, Showaddywaddy, Patti Boulaye and Marti Caine. The show was revived in the 1980s but didn't have the same appeal.

Blankety Blank was first introduced to audiences on 18 January 1979. It was hosted by Terry Wogan and included a panel on celebrities who completed sentences with what they thought would be the most popular answer. Regular panel members included Kenny Everett, Lorraine Chase, Gareth Hunt, Gary Davies, and Cheryl Baker. It was a hit with the viewing public and continued until 1990 with a variety of hosts including Les Dawson and Lily Savage.

Early dramas of the 1970s included Callan (1967-72) starring Edward Woodward, Randall and Hopkirk (1969-70) and Department S (1969-70).

For children, there was Animal Magic (1962-83), Doctor Who (1963-present), Play School (1964-88), Jackanory (1965-96), Magpie

The Waltons was an incredible success during the 1970s and pulled in millions of viewers. The show starred Ralph Waite (John Walton), Richard Thomas (John-Boy) and Michael Learned (Olivia Walton).

(1968-80), The Clangers (1969-74), Screen Test (1969-84), Andy Pandy (1950-70) and Scooby Doo, Where Are You (1969-70).

Entertainment shows included the popular Black and White Minstrel Show (never to be seen again), The Good Old Days, The Paul Daniels' Magic Show and the chat show, Parkinson, hosted by Michael Parkinson and featuring some of the biggest names of the day.

Moses the Lawgiver was broadcast between 1973 and 1974 and starred Burt Lancaster in the title role. It was a huge production and featured six one-hour episodes. It also starred Anthony Quayle, Ingrid Thulin and Irene Papas and featured music by Ennio Morricone. The same production crew were later responsible for Jesus of Nazareth.

American programmes also played a big part during the 1970s including The Waltons which was broadcast throughout the decade and was a favourite with many people. It told the story of the lives of the Walton family in rural Virginia during the Great Depression and the

David Carradine and Sondra Locke in the hit tv show, Kung Fu. The show was hugely successful and ran between 1972 and 1975.

Second World War. The pilot show, 'The Homecoming: A Christmas Story', was first aired in 1971 and the series ran from September 1972 for nine seasons before it was cancelled in 1981. However, movie sequels were broadcast in the 1990s. The story revolved around John Walton Jr (John-Boy) and his family which included his six brothers and sisters, his parents John and Olivia Walton, and his grandparents Zebulon (Zeb) and Esther Walton. John-Boy was the oldest of the children and later became a journalist and novelist. The opening of each episode was narrated by a middle-aged John-Boy and was voiced by author Earl Hamner.

Kung Fu, starring David Carradine, ran from 1972 until 1975 and told the story of Kwai Chang Caine, a Shaolin monk who was on the run from the Chinese authorities for the killing of the Emperor's nephew. Most of the action took place in America during the late 1800s and featured martial arts combined with the usual gunfights of

Henry Winkler as Arthur Fonzarelli (The Fonz) in Happy Days pictured with Ron Howard as Richie Cunningham. The show was a huge success both in the US and the UK.

the Wild West. Caine searched each week for his half brother, Danny Caine, before finally finding him at the end of the series. The show was very successful and was shown worldwide and made David Carradine a huge star. The show returned in 1993 and ran until 1997 but wasn't as popular as it had been in the 1970s.

In 1974 the Fonz was introduced to audiences in the ever-popular Happy Days starring Henry Winkler. It told the story of a 1950s family and their cool tenant, Arthur Fonzarelli. The series ran from 1974 until 1984 and was one of the decade's highest-rated series. It went on to spawn an equally popular half-hour comedy series, Mork and Mindy which starred Pam Dawber and Robin Williams.

Rhoda, starring Valerie Harper, was set in a New York tenement and featured the ups and downs of the title character. Julie Kavner (later the voice of Marge Simpson) played her erstwhile sister. It aired between 1974 and 1978.

The main stars of Rhoda: Julie Kavner (Brenda Morgenstern), Valerie Harper (Rhoda Morgenstern Gerard) and Nancy Walker (Ida Morgenstern).

The American tv series M*A*S*H ran between 1972 and 1983 and was based on the movie of the same name. The tv show starred Alan Alda and Wayne Rogers as Captain Hawkeye Pierce and Trapper John McIntyre, two army surgeons based at a Mobile Army Surgical Hospital during the Korean War. The show was a comedy and played with a laughter track in the US but this was removed in the UK. With its often dark humour and poignant story lines, it became one of the most popular shows of the 1970s and a record breaking 125 million people watched the final show. Also appearing in the first series were Loretta Swit (Margaret 'Hot Lips' Houlihan), Jamie Farr (Max Klinger), William Christopher (Father Mulcahy), McLean Stevenson (Henry Blake), Larry Linville (Frank Burns) and Gary Burghoff (Radar O'Reilly). The cast changed over the years introducing new characters and actors.

The stars of the television show, Planet of the Apes. Cast members included Roddy McDowall, Ron Harper and James Naughton and was first broadcast in 1974.

After the huge success of *Planet of the Apes* at the cinema, it was decided to make a television series featuring the movie's lead actor, Roddy McDowall. It was first broadcast in 1974. The show starred Ron Harper and James Naughton who played two astronauts who crash on a future earth. They are aided in their adventures by a chimpanzee called Galen, played by McDowall, while pursued by a band of gorillas led by their leader, Urko (Mark Lenard). The show was meant to run for fourteen episodes but was cancelled after thirteen due to low ratings in the US. However, it was hugely popular in Britain. A cartoon series, Return to the Planet of the Apes was shown the following year.

Soap (1977) featured the everyday chaotic lives of the Tates and the Campbells. Much of the comedy was whacky and hilarious and was a spoof of the many serious soaps that appeared on American tv at the time. One of the funniest characters was Burt (played by Richard Mulligan) who in later episodes was kidnapped by aliens and replaced with 'Alien Burt'. Memorable characters include Jessica Tate (Katherine Helmond) and her husband, Chester (Robert Mandan), Benson (Robert Guillaume) the sarcastic butler, Jodie (Billy Crystal) the gay son, Chuck (Jay Johnson) a ventriloquist and Mary Campbell (Cathryn Damon) the sister of Jessica Tate. Apart from alien abduction, the show included demonic possession, murder, insanity, a faked death, a cult and blackmail. Each show began with a recap of the previous episode and the words, 'Confused? You won't be, after this week's episode of...Soap.'

Taxi (1978) followed the lives of the employees of the fictional Sunshine Cab Company based in Manhattan. It featured the disillusioned Alex Reiger (Judd Hirsch), single mother Elaine Nardo (Marilu Henner), boxer Tony Banta (Tony Danza), struggling actor Bobby Wheeler (Jeff Conaway), aging hippie Reverend Jim Ignatowski (Christopher Lloyd), Latka Gravas (Andy Kaufman) and despotic dispatcher Louie De Palma (Danny DeVito). The show went on to win eighteen Emmy Awards and is fondly remembered. It made stars of many of its cast particularly Danny DeVito and Andy Kaufman.

Detective dramas proved hugely popular and there were many of these shown during the decade. These included Kojak, Columbo,

One of the biggest detective dramas of the 1970s, Starsky and Hutch. The show starred David Soul and Paul Michael Glaser as Ken Hutchinson and Dave Starsky. The programme also featured the memorable Huggy Bear (Antonio Fargas).

McMillan and Wife, Tenafly, Banacek, McCloud, Baretta, Barnaby Jones, Cannon, Starsky and Hutch, The Rockford Files, Police Woman, Police Story, Mannix, Madigan, The Streets of San Francisco, Hawaii 5-0, Charlie's Angels and Chips. There were many more.

Kojak, starring Telly Savalas, was a huge success and turned its star into an unexpected sex symbol. His trademark sunglasses, hat and lollipop were copied by impressionists (and children) everywhere as were his well-known catchphrases; 'Who Loves Ya Baby?' and 'Cootchie-coo!'.

Starsky and Hutch produced the same fan appeal as David Cassidy and Donny Osmond had earlier in the decade. Two good-looking cops, Dave Starsky and Ken Hutchinson, tore around the streets of Bay City, California in Starsky's Gran Torino, involving much action and memorable characters such as Huggy Bear and Captain Dobie. It ran from 1975 until 1978 and was hugely popular. As soon as the show was shown, its stars David Soul and Paul Michael Glaser were mobbed wherever they went. When David Soul travelled to Britain to make the movie *Mud* in 1976, he arrived by plane to receive the same adulation that Cassidy and Osmond had received some years previously. Posters of the duo appeared in teenagers' bedrooms everywhere, fanzines and magazines were sold in their thousands and endless programmes featured interviews with the lovable detectives. The show also led on to David Soul's successful singing career.

The UK's answer to the wealth of American police dramas was The Sweeney and The Professionals as well as already established shows such as Z Cars, Softly, Softly and Dixon of Dock Green.

The Sweeney ran between 1975 and 1978 and starred John Thaw as Detective Inspector Jack Regan and Dennis Waterman as his sidekick, Detective Sergeant George Carter. The hard-hitting show proved extremely popular with viewers. The programme was felt to be more realistic than previous cosy home-grown police dramas such as Dixon of Dock Green and Z Cars. The show was more violent and featured crooks, corruption and car chases. Anyone who was anyone at the time seemed to appear in guest roles in the show including Diana Dors, John Hurt, Patrick Troughton and Morecambe and Wise. It's worth watching nowadays just for the sight of classic 1970s cars as well as the huge flares worn by Carter and Regan.

In 1976, the American tv series Rich Man, Poor Man was first broadcast. It was based on a novel by Irwin Shaw and achieved great success. It starred Peter Strauss, Nick Nolte and Susan Blakely and told the story of the Jordache brothers. Rudy (Peter Strauss) was well-educated and ambitious while his brother, Tom (Nick Nolte), rebelled against everything. Their enemy, Falconetti (played by William Smith), was intent on killing both of them and appeared later in the series. The first series spanned a twenty-year period covering the time between 1945 and 1965. A follow up series continued the story in 1968.

The Dukes of Hazzard was easy viewing for Saturday nights featuring the adventures of the Duke Boys, who were cousins Bo Duke (John Schneider) and Luke Duke (Tom Wopat). The show also featured their attractive female cousin Daisy (Catherine Bach).

Lynda Carter as Wonder
Woman. The show
ran between 1975 and
1979 and starred Lynda
Carter as Diana Prince
(Wonder Woman) and
Lyle Waggoner as Steve
Trevor.

The show had a star car, The General Lee, and a host of memorable characters such as Boss Hogg and Sheriff Rosco P. Coltrane. The show drew a lot from the popular Burt Reynolds movies of the time.

Superheroes started to appear in tv programmes during the 1970s and the most popular of these were The Six Million Dollar Man (1973), Wonder Woman (1975), Spiderman (1977), The Bionic Woman (1976), The Man from Atlantis (1977) and The Incredible Hulk (1978).

The Six Million Dollar Man starred Lee Majors as former astronaut, Colonel Steve Austin, who, after being badly injured, is rebuilt using bionic limbs which give him superhuman strength. The show was hugely popular and lasted for three years. It led to a similar show, The Bionic Woman, which starred Lindsay Wagner as Jamie Sommers, a professional tennis player, who becomes seriously injured during a skydiving accident. With bionic repairs she finds herself working for Oscar Goldman as a secret agent. Steve Austin plays her on/off boyfriend throughout the series.

The Man from Atlantis starred Patrick Duffy, who would later play Bobby Ewing in Dallas. His role was that of the only surviving citizen of the lost civilization of Atlantis who possessed exceptional abilities, such as being able to breathe underwater.

Bill Bixby played Dr Bruce Banner, a scientist who, after being hit by gamma rays turns into the Incredible Hulk whenever he becomes upset. His catchline each week was 'Don't make me angry, you wouldn't like me when I'm angry!' The Hulk was played by Lou Ferrigno who looked huge at the time but today, with so many bodybuilders around, doesn't look quite as big as he once did.

While America had sci-fi shows such as Logan's Run (1977), Battlestar Galactica (1978) and Buck Rogers in the 25th Century (1979), Britain had Blake's 7 (1978) and Space 1999 (1975). Logan's Run featured a future world where no one lived longer than 30 years old. Gregory Harrison (as Logan 5) and Heather Menzies (as Jessica 6) escape and are pursued by Randy Powell (Francis 7). The tv show was based on the successful movie of the same name and lasted for fourteen episodes before it was cancelled.

Battlestar Galactica cashed in on the success of the movie, *Star Wars* and most of the action took place on a spaceship. The show starred Lorne Greene and Richard Hatch and involved the characters' war with a race of robots called the Cylons. The show returned in 1980 but, to save money, found itself earthbound.

Buck Rogers in the 25th Century starred Gil Gerard as the title character and also featured Erin Gray and Wilfrid Hyde-White. Many of the props and costumes were recycled from Battlestar Galactica, which was still being made at the time. The story tells of an astronaut, Buck Rogers, who after being launched in his spacecraft in May 1987 finds himself frozen for 504 years before his spacecraft is discovered in the year 2491.

Less hi-tech and far cheaper was the BBC's Blake's 7 which featured seven renegades and their adventures in a stolen spaceship.

Gareth Thomas played Blake, Paul Darrow played Avon and Michael Keating played Vila. Wobbly sets aside, it was incredibly popular and was watched by 10 million people in the UK. Clive James described it as 'classically awful'. The show ran between 1978 and 1981 and was created by Terry Nation, who also wrote scripts for Doctor Who.

Space 1999 was made in England but featured well-known American actor Martin Landau. A Gerry Anderson production, it told the story of an explosion on the moon in the year 1999. The occupants of Moonbase Alpha found themselves rocketed into outer space where they encountered many strange alien creatures. The show also featured Landau's wife, Barbara Bain. Lew Grade insisted that the main characters were American, to appeal to an international market, however, Gerry Anderson had wanted British stars. The show was popular with audiences but was described as wooden by some critics. It attracted a host of big names playing various characters including Christopher Lee, Roy Dotrice, Joan Collins, Peter Cushing, Judy Geeson, Julian Glover, Leo McKern, Patrick Troughton and David Prowse.

During 1976 Patrick Macnee revised his role as John Steed and appeared in a new series The New Avengers. The show also starred two assistants, Joanna Lumley as Purdey and Gareth Hunt as Gambit. It featured many of the storylines of the original 1960s series with the agents fighting evil plots and world domination, while featuring lots of karate kicks and twirling umbrellas. The show was a success and lasted two series.

In 1977 ITV first broadcast The Professionals which starred Martin Shaw, Lewis Collins and Gordon Jackson as agents working for the fictional CI5. The stars had already found fame in other programmes. Gordon Jackson was known for his role as Hudson in the popular Upstairs, Downstairs (1971), Lewis Collins appeared as Gavin in the comedy The Cuckoo Waltz (1975) (which also starred Diane Keen) and Martin Shaw had had parts in Doctor in the House (1969-1970), Coronation Street and The New Avengers (1976), with his future co-star Lewis Collins. The Professionals was seen as competition to the BBC's hugely popular show Starsky and Hutch. It shared the realism of The Sweeney and famously featured Ford

Capris as well as other classic 1970s cars including a Ford Granada (Cowley's car), a Ford Escort RS2000 (driven by Doyle) as well as a Rover SD1, a Rover P6, a Princess, a Triumph 2000, a Triumph Dolomite Sprint and a Triumph TR7. The series was criticised for its level of violence which included shootings and martial arts. Moral crusader Mary Whitehouse called the show both racist and sexist. It ended in 1983 and ITV replaced it with Dempsey and Makepeace. The show was remade starring Edward Woodward in the role of Cowley but it wasn't successful.

Alex Haley's Roots became the biggest and most popular television series of 1977. It told the story of Kunte Kinte who, in 1750, is taken from his homeland in The Gambia, West Africa, captured and sold to a slave trader before being transported to America. There, he is sold to a plantation owner, John Reynolds (played by Lorne Greene) and given the name Toby. The series was upsetting and often brutal and told of the lives and hardships of Kunte Kinte (played by LeVar Burton) and his descendants. Memorable characters included Kizzy (Leslie Uggams), Chicken George (Ben Vereen) and Mathilda (Olivia Cole). A sequel was aired in 1979 and featured highly respected actors of the day including Henry Fonda, Richard Thomas, Olivia de Havilland, Marlon Brando, Robert Culp and James Earl Jones.

Another huge hit of 1977 was Jesus of Nazareth which starred Robert Powell in the title role. The drama featured an all-star cast including Anne Bancroft, Ernest Borgnine, Laurence Olivier, Christopher Plummer, Anthony Quinn, Rod Steiger, and Peter Ustinov. The production was timed so that it was shown over the Easter period.

In 1978 one of the most popular, not-to-be-missed, shows on television was Dallas which told the story of an American oil-rich family and all the dramas that went with their day-to-day lives. The series started with the marriage of Bobby Ewing and Pamela Barnes. Their families were sworn enemies in the oil business. Bobby's brother, J.R., threw a spanner in the works at every turn with his various schemes and dirty deals. The cliff-hanger at the end of the 1970s involved the shooting of J.R. and a huge campaign was launched with the slogan 'Who Shot JR?'. Storylines at the time were kept secret and the episodes arrived in the UK by plane under guard so no one knew what was going to happen until the episode was broadcast.

Other popular characters in the show included Jock Ewing (Jim Davis), the head of the family; Miss Ellie (Barbara Bel Geddes), his wife; Sue Ellen (Linda Gray), J.R.'s alcoholic wife; Lucy (Charlene Tilton), Jock's granddaughter; and Pam's brother Cliff (Ken Kercheval). People were hooked by the twists and turns of the Ewing family but it started to lose its appeal after the death of Bobby Ewing. He later returned to the show and it was explained that the whole previous series had been a 'dream'. This was too much for even the most ardent viewers, but still it continued. In 1979, Dallas spawned an off-shoot, Knot's Landing.

Meanwhile in the UK, comedy proved to be a huge hit. The Good Life (1975) told the story of Tom and Barbara Good who lived a self-sufficient life at their home in Surbiton much to the amusement of their middle-class neighbours, Margot and Jerry Leadbetter. The show starred Richard Briers, Felicity Kendal, Penelope Keith and Paul Eddington and was written by John Esmonde and Bob Larbey. It ran until 1978 and became one of the UK's favourite comedy shows.

Fawlty Towers (1975) is one of the best-remembered comedies of the decade. It starred John Cleese as the abrasive, Basil Fawlty, who owned a run-down hotel in Torquay. The chaotic life of Fawlty is best displayed in the episode 'The Germans' where he keeps reminding his German guests of the war with hilarious results. Also appearing in the show each week was Prunella Scales as Basil's wife Sybil, Connie Booth as chambermaid Polly and Andrew Sachs as hapless waiter Manuel. The show also featured the confused Major Gowen played by Ballard Berkeley. The show was based on a real hotel manager whom the stars of Monty Python had met some years previously while staying in Devon.

The Fall and Rise of Reginald Perrin (1976) was one of the best British comedies of the 1970s and starred Leonard Rossiter (previously seen in the excellent ITV series Rising Damp) in the title role. His downtrodden character is disillusioned in his managerial job at Sunshine Desserts working for the overpowering CJ, who is best remembered for the phrase, 'I didn't get where I am today...'. Chaotic twists and turns eventually lead to Perrin faking his own death with hilarious results. The show ran for three series but lost its way after series two. It was later remade and starred Martin Clunes in a poor imitation of the original.

In the UK, in 1978, one of the BBC's most popular dramas was All Creatures Great and Small which told the story of a vet and his adventures assisting in a practice in Yorkshire. The series was based on the popular books written by James Herriot and featured Christopher Timothy as the lead character, at the time Timothy was better known for his appearances on television adverts promoting *The Sun* newspaper. Also appearing in the show was Robert Hardy as the abrasive Siegfried Farnon, Peter Davison as Siegfried's younger brother, Tristan and Carol Drinkwater as Helen Herriot. The show continued until 1990.

Minder (1979) starred Dennis Waterman as Terry McCann who was employed as a bodyguard to the unscrupulous businessman, Arthur Daley. The show involved dodgy dealings and much fighting with Waterman's character usually coming off the worst. It was very successful.

By the end of the 1970s, television had moved on a great deal since the beginning of the decade. Most families now had a colour television, some had the latest video recorders, while many used their sets to play the video game Pong which was a very basic tennis game. Video recorders were also beginning to be introduced complete with basic wired-in remote controls, something unheard of in the UK previously.

There were many, many more excellent television programmes shown during the 1970s and although many are today lampooned for being sometimes crass, racist or sexist, they formed the basis of many similar shows that we watch today.

Celebrity quotes:

'*You cannot represent cool. You've got to be cool. You've got to be authentic. I think, after all these years, that is how I define cool. It is being authentic. That is powerful.*' Henry Winkler (The Fonz).

'*I have no regrets about being 'Doctor Who'. It was the greatest thing that ever happened to me.*' Tom Baker.

'*Paul (Michael Glaser) and I were both struggling actors. One night he would serve me in a restaurant, and the next night I would serve him. It was what out of work actors did.*' David Soul.

'*It would almost be sinful to say that I regretted doing 'Charlie's Angels' because it did so much for my career.*' Farrah Fawcett.

'*I think JR would make a better President than the one we have now.*' Larry Hagman.

Chapter 5

Movies

Undoubtedly, the most talked about movie of the 1970s was *Star Wars*. Its revolutionary special effects spawned many imitators and a host of space-based films and television shows followed. Movies included *Close Encounters of the Third Kind*, *The Black Hole*, *Capricorn One*, *Star Crash* and *Star Trek* while television programmes included Blake's 7, Buck Rogers in the 25th Century and Battlestar Galactica. No copies had the longevity or the success of the original and the movie made a huge star of one of its key players, Harrison Ford. The franchise continues today with everyone knowing who Darth Vader, C3PO and R2D2 are. When the film was released in 1977, it was long

The Dominion Theatre showing the hugely successful *Star Wars*. The movie was first shown in 1977 and became one of the most popular films of all time.

awaited and much talked about. The special effects, at the time, were revolutionary and cinema goers became lost in 'a galaxy far, far away'.

The final years of the 1970s gave way to sci-fi films with *Close Encounters of the Third Kind* (1977) and *Superman* (1978) becoming box office hits. Marlon Brando's £4 million cameo in *Superman* was much discussed and wondered at and Christopher Reeve's flying sequences as the superhero, at the time, seemed amazing. Cinema was entering a new era of special effects long before digital took over.

Close Encounters of the Third Kind fuelled imaginations everywhere and suddenly, as with the X Files in later years, there was a huge rise in reports of UFO sightings and alien abductions.

Earlier in the decade, the most popular films, as with television, featured detectives. These included *The French Connection, Dirty Harry* and *Shaft*, all released in 1971. *The French Connection*

Richard Roundtree, the cool star of the detective drama, *Shaft*. The original movie was released in 1971 when detective movies were at their height.

introduced Popeye Doyle, a New York Police Department detective, played brilliantly by Gene Hackman. It won the Academy Award not just for best film, but also for best actor and best director.

Dirty Harry featured the laconic Clint Eastwood in the title role as a detective based in San Francisco who employed some unorthodox methods, and a Magnum 44, to get his man. The movie spawned four sequels: *Magnum Force* (1973), *The Enforcer* (1976), *Sudden Impact* (1983) and *The Dead Pool* (1988). The film is remembered for the catchphrase 'Make my day' as much as it is for the action and story. There was controversy when the film was released because of its police brutality, it was a huge success, however, and *Time* magazine praised Eastwood by saying that he 'gave his best performance so far, tense, tough, full of implicit identification with his character.' Today, it is considered one of the best movies of 1971.

Other detective movies included *Shaft* (starring Richard Roundtree) and *Serpico* (starring Al Pacino). *Shaft* was followed by two more films in the series which were *Shaft's Big Score* (1972) and *Shaft in Africa* (1973), but neither was as successful as the first. *Shaft* later resurfaced in a series of seven tv movies shown between 1973 and 1974.

War films such as Francis Ford Coppola's *Patton* (starring George C. Scott) and Robert Altman's *M*A*S*H*, proved to be major box-office draws in 1970. Romantic movies such as *Love Story* (1970) and *Summer of '42* (1971) were huge commercial successes and two of the most profitable Hollywood movies of the time.

Westerns continued to be popular in the 1970s and had been a firm favourite at the cinema for many decades. These included *Little Big Man, A Man Called Horse, Soldier Blue, Rooster Cogburn* and *The Outlaw Josey Wales. Soldier Blue* caused controversy when it was released in 1970 for its portrayal of the slaughter of Native American Indians. The film starred Peter Strauss (who would later find fame in the television series Rich Man, Poor Man) and Candice Bergen. The movie was the third most popular at the British box office when it was released in 1971. Although it was extremely successful in the UK and around the world, it wasn't quite so in the US where the

Warner in the West End showing three of the popular movies of the 1970s including *The Outlaw Josey Wales, All the President's Men* and *St Ives* starring Charles Bronson.

groundbreaking violence showing the cavalry's violence towards its native people was a bit too close to what was happening in Vietnam at the time.

A Clockwork Orange was released in 1971 and starred Malcolm McDowell. Its violent, graphic images of gang culture led to it being banned in 1972 and it didn't appear in cinemas again until 1999. The movie was blamed for copycat murders and attacks and was deemed not suitable for the general public.

Sean Connery returned to the role of James Bond in 1971, after a short stint where the character was played by George Lazenby. *Diamonds Are Forever* proved to be Connery's last film in the series (although he did return much later in *Never Say Never Again*). The role was taken over by Roger Moore who was famous on television for his roles as Simon Templar in The Saint and as the title character in Ivanhoe. Moore's first Bond movie was *Live and Let Die* which was released in 1973. The film featured one of the best Bond themes ever, performed by Paul McCartney and Wings. The movie proved totally

The suave Roger Moore star of the James Bond movies of the 1970s. His first appearance in the role was in *Live and Let Die* (1973) which also starred Jane Seymour.

different from the Sean Connery films and Roger Moore soon made the role his own. Today it is worth watching just for the crazy 1970s fashions including flared trousers and platform shoes. The movie was followed up with *The Man With the Golden Gun* in 1974 which starred Christopher Lee in the role of Scaramanga. Hervé Villechaize played his loyal assistant, Nick Nack. He would later appear in a very similar role in the US television series, Fantasy Island. Amazingly, *The Man With the Golden Gun* made the least profit of a Bond film at the box office although it had everything that was expected of a Bond movie. There was a long break before the series returned again in 1977 with *The Spy Who Loved Me*. The last Bond movie of the decade was *Moonraker* which was released in 1979. It became the highest grossing Bond film until *Golden Eye* was released in 1995. The box office takings for *Moonraker* seem odd as it contained one of the weaker stories of all the Bond films.

In 1972 one of the best remembered films of the decade, *The Godfather*, was released. It starred Marlon Brando as the head of the Corleone family and featured some of the decade's biggest names including Al Pacino, James Caan and Robert Duvall. Brando received an Academy Award for best actor. It paved the way for further gangster type movies including, inevitably, *Godfather Part II* (1974), *Mean Streets* (1973), *Dillinger* (1973) and *Capone* (1975).

In the same vein but with a lighter feel came *The Sting* (1973) which reunited Robert Redford and Paul Newman as a pair of conmen preparing for their biggest hit. Robert Shaw played a major role in the movie and would later play a big part in the film *Jaws*.

Westworld in 1973 combined sci-fi and westerns and featured Yul Brynner as an out-of-control robot in a Wild West theme park. Brynner recreated a role that he'd played in *The Magnificent Seven* but with more deadly effect. The film proved highly entertaining and led to a follow-up, *Future World* (1976) which starred Peter Fonda and Blythe Danner. Yul Brynner made a cameo appearance in a dream sequence.

The *Planet of the Apes* franchise continued throughout the 1970s. The original movie had been released in 1968 and its sequel *Beneath the Planet of the Apes* was released in 1970. The film was, perhaps, the worst of the series and is little shown nowadays but still proved a big hit at the box office. *Escape from the Planet of the Apes* was released the following year and showed two of the main characters from the previous films. Cornelius (played by Roddy McDowall) and Zira (Kim Hunter) escape to present day earth in the spaceship that had crashed in their time in the original movie. It was well received and led on to two more films *Conquest of the Planet of the Apes* (1972) and *Battle for the Planet of the Apes* (1973). The final film made the least money and received poor reviews, however, a television series was commissioned in 1974 but ended after one series amid low viewing figures.

In 1973 one movie appeared in the newspapers regularly with endless stories of attempted suicides and breakdowns. The movie was *The Exorcist* which starred Linda Blair as a demon-possessed 12-year-old girl. Many called for it to be banned. Its incredible success led to four sequels but also inspired movies such as *The Omen* (1976) starring

The Rocky Horror Show at the King's Road Theatre. The movie was released in 1975 and was based on the popular stage show written by Richard O'Brien who also played Riff Raff in the production. The movie also starred Tim Curry and Susan Sarandon.

Gregory Peck and *Carrie* (1976) which starred Sissy Spacek and was based on the Stephen King novel.

Musicals also proved popular throughout the 1970s and included *Cabaret* (1972), *Jesus Christ Superstar* (1973), *Tommy* (1975), *Funny Lady* (1975) – a sequel to the 1968 movie *Funny Girl*, *The Rocky Horror Picture Show* (1975), *A Star in Born* (1976) *New York, New York* (1977) and *All That Jazz* (1979).

Jesus Christ Superstar was released in 1973 and starred Ted Neeley in the lead role. The production was written by Andrew Lloyd Webber and Tim Rice and had played on stage since 1970. Some religious groups claimed the movie was blasphemous but overall, it received

Sylvester Stallone who found fame in *Rocky* in 1976. The movie proved incredibly popular and led to several sequels. The original film also starred Talia Shire as Adrianna 'Adrian' Pennino and Burgess Meredith as Mickey Goldmill.

a great reception and was a huge success. Towards the end of the decade, there was one more film featuring the story of Jesus which, again caused an uproar from religious groups and there was a call for it to be banned. Monty Python's *Life of Brian* was released in 1979 and took a light-hearted view on the subject but it didn't go down too well in many quarters.

Sylvester Stallone found fame as Rocky Balboa in *Rocky* in 1976. The film told of the rags to riches tale of a boxer who starts out as a small-time fighter but ends up competing in the world heavyweight championship. The film also starred Talia Shire and Burgess Meredith as Rocky's trainer. It became the highest grossing film of 1976 and won three Oscars. The film was followed by six sequels including *Rocky II*, released in 1979.

Robert De Niro also found fame in 1976 appearing as a lone vigilante, Travis Bickle who becomes obsessed with Betsy, a campaign volunteer for Senator Charles Palantine whom he later tries to kill. The movie also starred Cybill Shepherd as Betsy and Jodie Foster as Iris.

John Travolta, star of both *Saturday Night Fever* (1977) and *Grease* (1978), both incredibly popular films in the late 1970s. Both movies produced many hit singles.

Taxi Driver directed by Martin Scorsese, went on to be nominated for four Academy Awards.

The huge hit of 1977 was *Saturday Night Fever* which starred John Travolta as Tony Manero, a 19-year-old who worked at a paint store. He came alive at the weekends, dancing at a Brooklyn discotheque. The movie featured music by the Bee Gees and the soundtrack became one of the biggest selling albums of all time. The movie was an incredible success.

The big musical hit of 1978 was *Grease* which, again, starred John Travolta and Olivia Newton-John as two love-sick teenagers in the 1950s, Danny Zuko and Sandy Olsson. The movie was the highest earner for the year and produced some of the most memorable hits in the chart that year including 'Summer Loving', 'Hopelessly Devoted to You' and 'You're the One That I Want'. The film cashed in on the resurgence of rock 'n roll music in the 1970s and television shows such as Happy Days.

Vietnam inspired movies included *The Deer Hunter* (1978) and *Apocalypse Now* (1979).

The huge blockbuster of 1975 was *Jaws*, directed by Steven Spielberg and starring Richard Dreyfuss, Roy Scheider and Robert Shaw, which told the story of a huge man-eating shark. It was so successful that it soon became the highest grossing film of all time until *Star Wars* was released in 1977. It was followed by three sequels, none of which were as good as the original. The movie won three Academy Awards and Spielberg shot to the top of his profession. For the summer of 1975, *Jaws* was the one movie that the general public, and beachgoers, talked about and still holds up against movies made today. Other movies were quickly made to jump on the bandwagon. These included *The Deep* (1977) starring Jacqueline Bisset and Nick Nolte and *Piranha* (1978) starring Bradford Dillman.

Disaster movies were very popular in the 1970s and drew huge audiences. Some of the best of these were *Airport* (1970), *The Poseidon Adventure* (1972) and *The Towering Inferno* (1974). There was also *Airport 1975* (1974), *Earthquake* (1974), *The Swarm* (1978), *Avalanche* (1978), *Meteor* (1979) and *Hurricane* (1979).

Airport was based on Arthur Hailey's novel and starred Burt Lancaster and Dean Martin. The story revolves around an airport manager continuing to run an airport while a snowstorm is in progress. Meanwhile, a suicidal bomber tries to blow up the Boeing 707 airliner while it is in flight. The movie was hugely successful and led to *Airport 1975* (which starred Charlton Heston), *Airport '77* (which starred George Kennedy, Jack Lemmon, James Stewart, Joseph Cotten and Olivia de Havilland) and *The Concorde ... Airport '79* (which starred, again, George Kennedy, Alain Delon and Robert Wagner). The last film was the worst of the series and brought the franchise to an end.

The sci-fi theme of the 1970s was rounded off at the end of the decade by *Alien* (1979), a first commercial success for director Ridley Scott, which starred Sigourney Weaver as Ripley an astronaut aboard

Dustin Hoffman who starred in 1970s hits *Straw Dogs* (1971), *Papillon* (1973), *All the President's Men* (1976) and *Kramer vs Kramer* (1979).

the spaceship Nostromo whose crew is stalked by an alien. Perhaps one of the most memorable scenes in the film is of an alien ripping out of the chest of John Hurt. The movie also starred Tom Skerritt, Harry Dean Stanton, Ian Holm, Veronica Cartwright and Yaphet Kotto. It was a huge success and spawned several sequels.

Other memorable movies of the 1970s included *All The President's Men* (1976) which starred Robert Redford and Dustin Hoffman as the journalists who uncovered the Watergate scandal; *Network* (1976) which starred Faye Dunaway, William Holden, Peter Finch and told the story of a failing television network; and *Kramer vs Kramer* (1979) which starred Dustin Hoffman and Meryl Streep as a divorced couple fighting over the custody of their boy. The film received five Academy Awards.

Manhatten and *Quadrophenia* showing at the ABC Classic in 1979.

There were many more incredible films made during the 1970s and movies such as *Star Wars* and James Bond continue to entertain audiences with continued new releases.

Celebrity quotes:

'An actor's a guy who, if you ain't talking about him, ain't listening.' Marlon Brando.

'I have always hated that damn James Bond. I'd like to kill him.' Sean Connery.

'Dancing's part of my soul. I enjoy it, it makes people happy, and it makes me happy.' John Travolta.

'Once a month the sky falls on my head, I come to and I see another movie I want to make.' Steven Spielberg.

'I enjoy being a highly overpaid actor.' Roger Moore.

Chapter 6

Sport

Some of the most iconic and best-remembered sports stars featured in the 1970s. In tennis, there was Virginia Wade, Björn Borg, Jimmy Connors, Ilie Năstase and later John McEnroe. Wimbledon was a huge attraction and warm sunny days in June were spent indoors watching tennis matches on the television. Many tuned in not just to watch good tennis but to watch the latest outbursts of Ilie Năstase or, later on, John McEnroe. McEnroe was very popular in the early 1980s, and every match he played was sure to feature an argument or outburst. Phrases like 'You can not be serious,' shouted by McEnroe to umpires and 'The ball was in' were well mimicked. However, for the 1970s, Ilie 'Nasty' Năstase was the bad boy of tennis, and, love him or hate him, he certainly brought in the viewers.

Björn Borg was the darling of the court and between 1974 and 1981, he became the first professional male tennis player to win eleven Grand Slam singles titles, which included six at the French Open and five consecutive wins at Wimbledon. By 1979 he was the first player to win more than $1 million in prize money in a single season.

On 1 July 1977 Virginia Wade won the women's singles championship at Wimbledon. She was ranked as number two in the world in women's singles and number one in the doubles. During 1977, with the Queen's Jubilee celebrations, Virginia Wade winning at Wimbledon seemed the icing on the cake and for a while Great Britain was on top of the world. Martina Navratilova won her first major singles title at Wimbledon in 1978 after defeating Chris Evert.

In athletics, famous names included David Bedford, Brendan Foster and Mary Peters.

Ilie Năstase, one of the world's top players in the 1970s who was ranked number one in the world during 1973 and 1974.

Björn Borg became the first professional tennis player to achieve eleven Grand Slam singles titles between 1974 and 1981.

Motor racing pin-up, James Hunt, winner of the Formula One World
Championship in 1976. He retired three years later in 1979.

The main celebrities of the day in motor racing, were James Hunt,
Jackie Stewart, Niki Lauda, Emerson Fittipaldi, Mario Andretti, Jody
Scheckter and Jochen Rindt. In 1970, Rindt won the Formula One
World Drivers' Championship but died in a crash in Monza later that
year. Previously he had won the 24-hour Le Mans race in 1965.

James Hunt was the pin-up of the racetrack and famously won the
Formula One World Championship in 1976. He retired from racing in
1979 and became a commentator and businessman. Hunt had joined
Formula One racing in 1973 and his exploits on the track earned him
the nickname 'Hunt the Shunt'. He raced for Hesketh before joining
the McLaren team in 1975 then joined the Wolf team in early 1979
before retiring.

Niki Lauda was an Austrian racing driver who was the Formula One champion three times in 1975, 1977 and 1984. He is the only champion who won the title racing for both McLaren and Ferrari. During the German Grand Prix in 1976, Lauda was seriously injured when his Ferrari burst into flames causing him severe burns. He recovered and returned to racing just six weeks later when he competed in the Italian Grand Prix. He had an on-track rivalry with James Hunt but they were close friends off the track.

Jackie Stewart competed in Formula One racing between 1965 and 1973 and won the championship in 1969, 1971 and 1973. In 1973, François Cevert, his Tyrrell team mate, was killed. Stewart had had his own brush with death in 1966 and had seen several of his friends killed in the sport. He retired from racing in 1973. Grand prix winners during the 1970s included Jackie Stewart (1971), Emerson Fittipaldi (1972), Jackie Stewart (1973), Emerson Fittipaldi (1974), Niki Lauda (1975), James Hunt (1976), Niki Lauda (1977), Mario Andretti (1978) and Jody Scheckter (1979). Jackie Stewart was nicknamed the Flying Scot and won three World Drivers' Championships between 1965 and 1973 while taking part in Formula One racing. He was runner-up twice over nine seasons.

During the 1970s, he became a sports commentator in America taking part in broadcasts for the Indianapolis 500, Daytona 500 and the Monaco Grand Prix from 1971 to 1986. He also covered the 1976 Winter and Summer Olympics for ABC Sports.

In 1970 Emerson Fittipaldi moved up from Formula Two to Formula One and made his debut for Lotus as a third driver at the British Grand Prix. Soon after, Jochen Rindt was killed at the 1970 Italian Grand Prix and Fittipaldi became Lotus's lead driver during his fifth Grand Prix. He was very successful while with Lotus and won the World Drivers' Championship in 1972. He was just 25 at the time, making him the youngest Formula One world champion, a record he held for thirty-three years. In 1974 he moved to McLaren and won the title again. Prior to the 1976 season, he moved to his brother's Fittipaldi Automotive team. He was replaced by James Hunt.

In 1974, Muhammad
Ali became heavyweight
champion of the world
after knocking out
George Foreman in Zaire
in a fight that became
known as the 'Rumble in
the Jungle'.

Mario Andretti, the 1978 World Champion, had a long career racing cars winning races in Formula One, IndyCar, World Sportscar Championship and NASCAR (The National Association for Stock Car Auto Racing).

Boxing stars of the day included Muhammad Ali, Henry Cooper, George Foreman and Joe Frazier. In 1970 Muhammad Ali returned to boxing three and a half years after being exiled for refusing to fight in the Vietnam War. He defeated Jerry Quarry by a third round technical knock out. On 8 March 1971 Ali was defeated by Joe Frazier at Madison Square Garden in a match which became known as 'The Fight of the Century'. By 1974, Muhammad Ali knocked out George Foreman in the eighth round in Zaire and became heavyweight world champion on 30 October. The match became known as the 'Rumble in the Jungle'. Also, on 1 October 1975, Ali beat Joe Frazier in a match in Manila known as the 'Thriller in Manila'.

Housewives' favourite, Jackie Pallo, one of the most popular wrestlers during the 1960s and 1970s. He had an onscreen rivalry with a fellow wrestler, Mick McManus.

In 1979 Sugar Ray Leonard won his first world boxing title. Leonard boxed in professional fights between 1977 and 1997. He won world titles in five different weight divisions as well as the lineal championship in three weight divisions and the undisputed welterweight title. In 1976, 1979 and 1981, the Boxing Writers Association of America (BWAA) named him Fighter of the Year.

Britain's John Conteh was hugely successful during the 1970s winning multiple light-heavyweight championships, including the WBC title from 1974 to 1978 as well as the European, British and Commonwealth titles between 1973 and 1974.

Grandstand and World of Sport were the key sporting television programmes in the UK during the time and were shown every Saturday afternoon.

World of Sport, hosted by Dickie Davies, was, perhaps, most popular for its wrestling bouts which began at 4pm. Stars of the day included Les Kellett, Jackie Pallo, Mick McManus, Big Daddy, Giant Haystacks, Kendo Nagasaki, Catweazle, The Royal Brothers and Steve Veidor. By 4pm on a Saturday, shops would empty as many people had returned home to watch the wrestling; it was all taken very seriously. Children and adults would shout at the television if there were any misdemeanours with cries of 'public warning!'. Everyone's favourite baddie was Mick McManus, complete with his jet-black boot-polish hair. When the wrestlers toured the country visiting various theatres, many were attacked by elderly women with their handbags totally believing that all of what they saw before them was real.

The wrestling was followed by the football results and men would check their pools coupons in the hope that this was the week they would get eight draws and be made millionaires. Before the lottery was introduced in the 1990s, doing the pools was your best chance of striking it rich. Some men's only sporting activity during the 1970s was filling in their pools coupon.

World of Sport also introduced the British public to Evel Knievel, a motorcycle stuntman from America. For a while, the world was Knievel crazy and merchandise and toys became very popular with children. His stunts were featured regularly on World of Sport, most memorably his failed leap over Snake River Canyon in 1974. During 1975 he appeared before 90,000 spectators at Wembley Stadium and attempted to jump over thirteen buses. He failed and smashed his pelvis. He managed to address the audience after the stunt and said, 'Ladies and gentlemen of this wonderful country, I've got to tell you that you are the last people in the world who will ever see me jump. Because I will never, ever, ever jump again. I'm through.' Amazingly, Knieval refused a stretcher and managed to walk off. But by October 1975 he was jumping again. This time he rode a motorcycle, successfully, leaping over fourteen Greyhound buses at Kings Island theme park near Cincinnati, Ohio. Knievel was said to have broken every bone in his body at one time or another.

Snooker and darts were also introduced to the viewing public through Saturday afternoon sport. In January 1979, over eight million viewers watched John Lowe beat Leighton Rees to win the Embassy World Professional Darts Championship. The competition was broadcast live on the BBC. Television made household names of many professional darts players and these included Eric Bristow, Alan Evans, Jocky Wilson and Cliff Lazarenko.

Snooker also became incredibly popular on television even when most people were still watching in black and white. Ray Reardon, a former policeman and miner, won six world titles during the 1970s. John Spencer and Alex 'Hurricane' Higgins were strong competitors and had celebrity status, especially Higgins for his bad boy image. Rising stars included Terry Griffiths and Steve Davis. Davis would win his first championship in 1980.

Four Olympic games (summer and winter) were held in the 1970s. The most memorable event of the earlier competition was the attack at the summer games in 1972 when Palestinian terrorists killed two Israeli hostages and held nine others captive. Olga Korbut won three gold medals for the Soviet Union in gymnastics in the same year and Mark Spitz won seven gold medals in the swimming events. The highlights of the 1976 Olympics in Montreal were Nadia Comăneci of Romania winning three gold medals in gymnastics, and the success of the US boxing team which won five gold medals. The team consisted of Sugar Ray Leonard, Leon Spinks, Michael Spinks, Leo Randolph and Howard Davis Jr.

Sharron Davies was selected to represent Great Britain at the 1976 Summer Olympics while only 13 years old. Although she didn't win any medals at the event, it made her a household name and she went on to win two bronze medals in 1977 in the European Championships

Bobby Moore receiving the World Cup from the Queen in 1966. Unfortunately,
England weren't so lucky in 1970. The overall winners at the beginning of the
decade were Brazil.

Fashion on the terraces in
the 1970s.

and gold medals in 1978 at the Commonwealth Games in both the 200 and 400 metre individual medleys, as well as picking up further silver and bronze medals.

In football, England hoped to repeat their 1966 success in the 1970 World Cup but were beaten in the quarter finals putting them in eighth position out of sixteen. The team featured some of England's greats such as Gordon Banks, Terry Cooper, Alan Mullery, Bobby Moore, Francis Lee, Alan Ball, Bobby Charlton, Geoff Hurst, Martin Peters and Peter Bonetti. World Cup fever could be seen everywhere in 1970. Esso gave away coins showing the heads of England's players, bubblegum cards, stickers and posters appealed to children, and the team released their own single 'Back Home' which went to number one where it stayed for three weeks. Everyone thought that England could win the title again but the eventual winners were Brazil, whose star player, Pelé, made up what was thought to be the greatest team of all time.

England failed to qualify in 1974 and 1978. Scotland became UK's hope for a win in 1978 but they were eliminated in the first stage. The World Cup was won by West Germany in 1974.

The first FA Cup winners of the decade were Chelsea who beat Leeds United 2-1 (after a replay). They were followed by Arsenal (1971), Leeds United (1972), Sunderland (1973), Liverpool (1974), West Ham United (1975), Southampton (1976), Manchester United (1977), Ipswich Town (1978) and Arsenal (1979).

The First Cricket World Cup was played in 1975. Famous cricketers of the 1970s included Derek Randall, Ian Botham, Ray Illingworth, Mike Gatting, David Gower and Graham Gooch. The England team, captained by Ray Illingworth, won the Ashes in 1971 and retained them the following year. The team also beat Pakistan at home before losing to India. This was probably one of England's strongest teams and included Boycott, Edrich, D'Oliveira, Amiss, Illingworth, Knott, Snow and Underwood.

Ray Illingworth and other members of his team refused to tour India and in 1973 and Illingworth was replaced by Mike Denness who lasted eighteen months in the job and lost the Ashes to the Australians during the 1974–1975 season.

In 1975 Denness was replaced by Tony Greig but they were beaten by the younger West Indies team the following year. Greig was eventually sacked and replaced by Mike Brearley. The side for the 1977 to 1980 team featured some great players including Ian Botham, David Gower and Graham Gooch and in 1978 England beat New Zealand 3-0 and Pakistan 2-0 before thrashing Australia 5-1 during the 1978 to 1979 season.

Rugby produced such stars as J.P.R. Williams, Gerald Davies, Gareth Edwards, Mervyn Davies and Barry John who were all part of the 1971 Lions team which returned triumphant from New Zealand. Wales won three Grand Slams in 1971, 1976 and 1978, six outright Five Nations titles and came close to beating the All Blacks in December 1972.

Bill Beaumont won thirty-four caps for England and was their captain twenty-one times during his career. As a 22-year-old, in 1975, he made his international debut in Dublin replacing Roger Uttley. Also in 1975, he went on to tour Australia followed by a tour of Japan, Fiji and Tonga in 1979. In 1981, he toured Argentina with the England team. He was part of the Barbarians team on fifteen occasions and took part in the match against the All Blacks in 1978. He was also part of the British Lions team to New Zealand in 1977. He replaced Nigel Horton who had broken his thumb. He went on to play in the three final tests. In 1978 he became the captain of the England team in Paris. He was also the captain of the North of England who beat the All Blacks in 1979.

Golf was also very popular with television viewers. Big names of the 1970s included Tony Jacklin who, in 1970, became the first British winner of the US Open for almost fifty years, at Hazeltine. Other star players included Jack Nicklaus (the winner of a total of eighteen major championships), Lee Trevino (winner of six major championships and twenty-nine PGA Tour events) and Gary Player (winner of nine major championships and six Champions Tour major championship victories). Nicklaus is considered to be the greatest golfer of all time.

Celebrity matches were shown regularly on the BBC and featured stars of the 1970s such as Telly Savalas, Ronnie Corbett, Jimmy Tarbuck, Bruce Forsythe and Dickie Henderson.

In horse racing, Nijinsky II won the Triple Crown of British Thoroughbred Racing in 1970. Red Rum won his third Grand National in 1977.

Some of the greatest and best-loved sporting personalities made their names in the 1970s and many inspired the sporting stars of today.

Celebrity quotes:

'*I hated every minute of training but I said, "Don't quit. Suffer now and live the rest of your life a champion".*' Muhammad Ali.

'*Muhammad Ali was a god, an idol and an icon. He was boxing. Any kid that had the opportunity to talk to Ali, to get advice from Muhammad Ali, was privileged. He's always given me time to ask questions, although I was so in awe that I didn't ask questions.*' Sugar Ray Leonard.

'*There's a lie that all drivers tell themselves. Death is something that happens to other people, and that's how you find the courage to get in the car in the first place. The closer you are to death the more alive you feel. But more powerful than fear itself, is the will to win.*' James Hunt.

'*I thought I was bulletproof or Superman there for a while. I thought I'd never run out of nerve. Never.*' Evel Knievel.

'*Whoever said,"It's not whether you win or lose that counts", probably lost.*' Martina Navratilova.

'*Even in moments of tranquillity, Murray Walker sounds like a man whose trousers are on fire.*' Clive James.

Celebrity Memory: Sharron Davies

I remember the crazy fashions of the 1970s including platform shoes and Oxford bags. At home, we had lino and Formica work surfaces and I remember Black Forest Gateaux and prawn cocktails. The blackouts during the miners' strikes stay in my memory. Although I was always training, the television programme that I loved was Starsky and Hutch. My memorable event of the 1970s was the 1976 Olympics when I was selected for the Summer Olympics at Montreal. I was just 13. My favourite mode of transport, at the time, was roller skates!

Chapter 7

UK Politics

Harold Wilson had been elected Prime Minister of Great Britain in October 1964 and stayed in the position until 19 June 1970 making him the first Prime Minister of the decade. He was succeeded by Edward Heath who ran the country until 4 March 1974 when Harold Wilson was once more elected. Wilson resigned as Prime Minister on 16 March 1976 and James Callaghan became Prime Minister on 5 April. He continued in the role until 4 May 1979, when Margaret Thatcher became Prime Minister and stayed in office until 28 November 1990, when John Major took over.

Harold Wilson had first entered parliament in 1945 and rose quickly before being elected as Leader of the Labour Party after the sudden death of Hugh Gaitskell in 1963. His period in office had seen low unemployment and economic prosperity. In 1969 he sent troops into Northern Ireland and lost the general election to Edward Heath during 1970. He spent the next four years as the Leader of the Opposition.

Edward Heath led the country from 1970 until 1974 under a Conservative government. In that time, he oversaw decimalisation in 1971 and reformed Britain's system of local government in 1972. In 1973 he took Britain into the European Community. He was Prime Minister during the height of The Troubles in Northern Ireland when he suspended the Stormont Parliament and imposed direct British rule.

Using the Industrial Relations Act 1971, Heath planned to curb the trade unions. A plan to deregulate the economy and transfer from direct to indirect taxation failed.

On 31 October 1971 the IRA exploded a bomb in the Post Office Tower in London. In 1972 secret talks were held with the IRA

The Conservatives took over government in 1970 and remained in power until 1974. Edward Heath faced many difficulties including the troubles in Northern Ireland and various industrial strikes.

leadership and a temporary ceasefire was agreed from 26 June to 9 July. Later in July the republicans met with Willie Whitelaw and turned down a peace deal because it didn't include a commitment to withdraw British troops or to release political prisoners.

Unemployment rose in 1972 and Heath attempted to control high inflation by a prices and incomes policy.

On 1 January 1973, the UK, the Republic of Ireland and Denmark entered the European Economic Community which would later become the European Union.

In 1972 and at the beginning of 1974, two miners' strikes took place which led to a three-day week with the aim of conserving energy. Television companies had to stop broadcasting at 10.30pm. Normal closing down times were restored on 23 February 1974. Commercial users of electricity were restricted to three days continuous use but essential services such as hospitals, as well as supermarkets and newspaper print works, were exempt.

The crisis began in October 1973 when Israel came under attack from the Arab states. The ensuing war in the Middle East meant that oil prices shot up and supplies to the west were reduced. At home, coal prices were rising and stocks were dwindling. After rejecting a pay increase, British miners voted to hold a national strike. On 12 November, the miners, together with electricity workers, imposed a ban on overtime. On 13 November, Edward Heath announced a state of emergency and electricity for non-essential use was banned. By staying neutral in the war between the Arab countries and Israel, Britain avoided the oil embargo that was imposed on the United States and Holland. Soon after, the post office issued petrol rationing books. By December, a 50 mph speed limit was imposed on all roads, offices could only be heated to 63 degrees Fahrenheit and there was an overall reduction in street lighting. Power cuts meant that many people had to get used to using candles for light and were unable to do little else, including watching television, until the electricity came back on.

On 13 December, the Prime Minister addressed the nation saying, 'As Prime Minister, I want to speak to you plainly about the grave emergency now facing our country. We are asking you to cut down to the absolute minimum the use of electricity in your homes.' He stated that there would be a three-day week from 1 January 1974 for industrial and commercial businesses as well as a 10.30pm closedown for television stations. However, Christmas television was to be exempt from this proposal. He went on to say, 'In terms of comfort we shall have a harder Christmas than we have known since the war.'

This damaged the government greatly and led to Edward Heath calling an election in February 1974. A hung-parliament resulted with Labour winning four more seats than the Conservatives but with fewer votes. Heath tried to form a coalition with the Liberal Party but this failed. He promised to continue as leader of the Conservatives, but in 1975 Margaret Thatcher challenged his leadership and became the party's new leader.

During 1974 Ross McWhirter – famous, together with his twin brother, Norris, as the co-founder of The Guinness Book of World Records and for his appearances on the BBC programme, Record Breakers – offered a £50,000 reward for information leading to the arrest of eight IRA bombers. He was later shot dead at his home. The same group later tried to kill Edward Heath.

Harold Wilson, the Prime Minister of Great Britain at the beginning of the decade and again between 1974 and 1976.

Meanwhile, the Labour leader, Harold Wilson, once more found himself leading the country. The Wilson government expanded the welfare state and increased spending on education, health and rent by imposing taxes on the rich. The new chancellor, Denis Healey, implemented an investment income surcharge raising the top rate on investment income to 98 per cent, which was the highest level since the Second World War. However, by 1975, unemployment had risen with 1,000,000 people out of work in Great Britain and inflation was rampant.

The Troubles continued in Northern Ireland. In February 1975 Merlyn Rees, the British Secretary of State for Northern Ireland, secured an IRA ceasefire. However, the ceasefire ended in January 1976. During November 1975 a bomb was planted by the IRA in a restaurant and exploded killing two people and injuring more than twenty others.

During 1975 Harold Wilson offered to pay Muammar Gaddafi, Libya's leader, £14 million to cease arming the IRA. However, Gaddafi demanded more which was unacceptable. The matter remained a secret until 2009.

James Callaghan who became Prime Minister when Harold Wilson resigned in 1976. He is remembered for the Winter of Discontent which took place during 1978 and 1979.

On 29 January 1976 twelve IRA bombs exploded in the West End of London. Four of the devices went off outside employment agencies while another was found inside Selfridge's department store in Oxford Street. A thirteenth bomb was found inside the record store, HMV. A taxi driver was injured during the explosions. For much of the day, Oxford Street was closed off while more bombs were searched for.

On 16 March 1976 Harold Wilson offered his resignation and was succeeded by James Callaghan who took office on 5 April 1976. Callaghan was the only politician ever to have served in the four major Offices of State. He was Chancellor of the Exchequer between 1964 and 1967, Home Secretary from 1967 to 1970 and Foreign Secretary from 1974, until he became Prime Minister in 1976. When Harold Wilson resigned, James Callaghan beat five other candidates to become the leader of the Labour party and the next Prime Minister. He remained leader of the party until 15 October 1980 although by then he had been succeeded by Margaret Thatcher as Prime Minister.

What became known as the Cod War ended on 1 June 1976, after an agreement between Iceland and the UK. In 1975, at a third United Nations Conference of the Law on the Sea, several countries agreed to a 185km limit of territorial waters. However, on 15 July 1975 the Icelandic government decided to extend its fishery limits and a third Cod War began which lasted between November 1975 and June 1976. Iceland extended its fishing limit to 370km and as a result there was conflict between British and Icelandic fishermen within the disputed zone. British fishermen had their nets cut by the Icelandic coastguard and there were several incidences of British trawlers being rammed by Icelandic ships. On 19 February 1976 it was announced by the British Minister of Agriculture, Fisheries and Food that the first British casualty of the Third Cod War was a fisherman from Grimsby who was seriously injured when a hawser hit him after Icelandic ships cut a trawl.

A total of twenty-two Royal Navy frigates were deployed to the area as well as seven supply ships, nine tug-boats and three support ships to protect the UK's fishing trawlers. Eventually, on 1 June 1976, after mediation through NATO, an agreement between Iceland and the UK was reached. Britain was allowed to keep twenty-four trawlers within the 200 nautical miles and fish a total of 30,000 tons.

James Callaghan was not unsuccessful as Prime Minister but is remembered for the 'Winter of Discontent' during 1978 and 1979 and his battles with trade unions which led to massive strikes which greatly affected the general public. On 4 November 1978, bakeries rationed bread after a nationwide bakers' strike. On 5 January 1979, lorry drivers took strike action and on 12 February a thousand schools closed after a heating oil shortage due to the lorry drivers' strike.

Airey Neave, the Shadow Secretary of State for Northern Ireland, was killed on 30 March 1979 by a car bomb planted outside the House of Commons. The bomb exploded as he drove out of the Palace of Westminster car park. The Irish National Liberation Army (INLA) later claimed responsibility. Before becoming a politician, Neave had been a British Army officer (he escaped from Colditz during the Second World War) and a barrister. Margaret Thatcher

Margaret Thatcher became the first female Prime Minister in 1979. She remained in the position until 1990.

said of Neave: 'He was one of freedom's warriors. No one knew of the great man he was, except those nearest to him. He was staunch, brave, true, strong; but he was very gentle and kind and loyal. It's a rare combination of qualities. There's no one else who can quite fill them. I, and so many other people, owe so much to him and now we must carry on for the things he fought for and not let the people who got him triumph.'

Prime Minister James Callaghan stated: 'No effort will be spared to bring the murderers to justice and to rid the United Kingdom of the scourge of terrorism.'

Two days prior to Airey Neave's assassination, a vote of no confidence in James Callaghan's government took place just weeks before the general election. Union problems, shortages and strikes ultimately led to Callaghan's downfall and he was defeated by Margaret Thatcher, who remained as Prime Minister between 4 May 1979 and 28 November 1990.

Margaret Thatcher would be forever known as 'Margaret Thatcher Milk Snatcher' after the withdrawal of school milk while she was Education Secretary at the beginning of the decade.

On being elected in 1979, Margaret Thatcher introduced a range of measures intended to reverse Britain's high unemployment, the effects of the Winter of Discontent and the increasing recession.

From 1970 until 1974, Margaret Thatcher had been the Education Secretary during Edward Heath's term as Prime Minister. She attracted public attention due to the administration's attempts to save money by cutting spending. Cuts led to the stopping of free milk for schoolchildren aged seven to eleven, earned Mrs Thatcher the nick-name, 'Margaret Thatcher, Milk Snatcher', although cabinet papers show that she opposed the policy. The newspapers and the Labour party demonised her for this, so much so that she considered leaving politics. As Leader of the Opposition between 1975 and 1979, she appointed Willie Whitelaw as her deputy.

In 1976 she gave her 'Britain Awake' foreign policy speech in which she lambasted the Soviet Union. This earned her the nickname 'Iron Lady'. The name arose after she gave a speech on foreign affairs and defence saying that the Soviets' aim was for world dominance. The journal of the Soviet Army, *Krasnaya Zvezda* (Red Star), disputed this in an article entitled, 'Iron Lady Raises Fears' which was written by Captain Yuri Gavrilov. The article suggested that Mrs Thatcher was similar to the 'Iron Chancellor' Bismarck of Imperial Germany. *The Sunday Times* picked up the Red Star article on the following day and, after Thatcher went on to mention the soubriquet 'Iron Lady' in a speech a week later, the name stuck.

Margaret Thatcher, together with Geoffrey Howe, her Chancellor of the Exchequer, reduced direct taxes on income and increased indirect taxes. She also increased interest rates with the aim of slowing the growth of the money supply and subsequently reducing inflation. Furthermore, she introduced cash limits on public spending and decreased expenditure on social services such as education and housing.

On 27 August 1979 Lord Mountbatten was assassinated by the IRA. Mountbatten had been lobster-potting and tuna fishing from his 30-foot wooden boat, *Shadow V*, which had been moored at Mullaghmore, County Sligo. The IRA had planted a bomb on the boat and detonated it while Mountbatten was on board, a few hundred yards from the shore. Fishermen pulled Mountbatten, aged 79, alive from the wreckage but he died soon after from his injuries. Also on board the boat were his eldest daughter Patricia (Lady Brabourne), her husband John (Lord Brabourne), their twin sons Nicholas and Timothy Knatchbull, John's mother Doreen, the dowager Lady Brabourne, and Paul Maxwell, a young crew member from County Fermanagh. Nicholas (aged 14) and Paul (aged 15) were killed by the explosion and the others were badly injured. Doreen,

Lady Brabourne, (aged 83) died from her injuries on the following day.

After the death of Mountbatten, the IRA issued a statement which read: 'The IRA claim responsibility for the execution of Lord Louis Mountbatten. This operation is one of the discriminate ways we can bring to the attention of the English people the continuing occupation of our country. The death of Mountbatten and the tributes paid to him will be seen in sharp contrast to the apathy of the British government and the English people to the deaths of over three hundred British soldiers, and the deaths of Irish men, women and children at the hands of their forces.'

On the day of the assassination of Lord Mountbatten, the IRA ambushed and killed eighteen British soldiers in Northern Ireland. Sixteen of them belonged to the Parachute Regiment. The attack became known as the Warrenpoint Ambush and was the deadliest attack on the British Army during the period of The Troubles.

On 16 November 1979, Sir Anthony Blunt was named as the fourth man in the Cambridge Spy Ring. At the time, Blunt was a leading British art historian. In 1964, after being offered immunity from prosecution, he confessed to having formerly been a Soviet spy as part of the Cambridge Five, a group of spies who worked for the Soviet Union between the 1930s and 1950s. The deception remained a secret for many years but was revealed by Margaret Thatcher in 1979 and he was stripped of his knighthood shortly afterwards. Margaret Thatcher was popular as Prime Minister at first but this waned with further recession and high unemployment. However, victory in the Falkland Islands in 1982 and a recovering economy increased her popularity and she went on to win the general election in 1983. However, her battle with the unions ultimately led to the Miners' Strike in 1984. She was re-elected Prime Minister in 1987 beating Labour's Neil Kinnock.

In politics, the decade is remembered for its numerous strikes, the black-outs, the many terrorist attacks carried out by the IRA, the end of the Cod War and the election of Britain's first female Prime Minister, Margaret Thatcher.

Celebrity quotes:

'*In politics a week is a very long time.*' Harold Wilson.

'*From out there on the Moon, international politics look so petty. You want to grab a politician by the scruff of the neck and drag him a quarter of a million miles out and say, "Look at that, you son of a bitch."*' Edgar Mitchell, Apollo 14 astronaut, (speaking in *People* magazine on 8 April 1974).

'*I don't think other people in the world would share the view there is mounting chaos.*' James Callaghan talking about the Winter of Discontent.

'*They have made a grave mistake choosing that woman.*' Edward Heath (on Margaret Thatcher's election to the leadership of the Tory Party, 1975).

'*Where there is discord, may we bring harmony. Where there is error, may we bring truth. Where there is doubt, may we bring faith. Where there is despair, may we bring hope.*' Margaret Thatcher (Quoting St Francis of Assisi, on her 1979 election victory).

Chapter 8

Innovations

In 1970, the first pocket calculator was invented in Japan. The first solid–state electronic calculator was made in the 1960s but pocket versions were possible because of the introduction of the first microprocessor, the Intel 4004, which was developed for Busicom, the Japanese calculator company. Calculators were soon mass produced. However, when they first came out, they had the restrictive price of about £150. This was soon reduced to £75 and they eventually became very cheap and were even given away free. Every schoolboy, office worker and businessman had to have one although many schools limited their use and still made pupils work out calculations using a pen and paper.

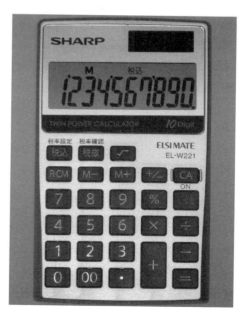

A Sharp pocket calculator. The first pocket calculator was introduced in the US in 1971 and were later mass produced and reduced in price.

Also in 1970, Sir Clive Sinclair developed one of the first handheld televisions, the MTV-1.

On 30 March 1970 the first home VCR was invented. However, it would still be a few years before most people in the UK would own one. At the beginning of the 1970s, the only way to watch the latest blockbusters at home was to have your own cine projector. Movies could be purchased in vastly shortened versions, many only lasting four minutes and often silent. There were also no video cameras and the only way to capture moving pictures was with a home movie cine camera which typically took Super 8mm film. It was grainy, needed a lot of light and was far from professional.

At the end of the 1970s home video recorders first appeared on the market to the British public. For the first time, people were able to record programmes while watching another, or tape programmes while they were out. It's commonplace nowadays but was a very novel invention back

A Pulsar digital watch. The watches were first sold in 1972 but were hugely expensive. Digital watches were later mass produced and became far cheaper in price.

in the 1970s. The first recorders were bulky and very expensive. At the time of introduction, a video recorder cost about £499. Video recorders had been around for a few years before but hardly anyone owned one. There were three basic formats when the home systems were introduced. These were the Phillips 2000, Betamax and VHS. All were incompatible with each other and by the 1980s, the VHS standard had won the race. By 1978 many consumers chose to rent a video recorder rather than buy one as the cost was prohibitive. Tape quality wasn't always great and many spun out and got stuck in the machine. Eventually, video recorders were superseded by the far superior DVD system.

In 1970 the first digital watch, a Pulsar LED prototype, was developed by Hamilton Watch Company and Electro-Data. The head of Hamilton's Pulsar division, John Bergey, revealed that he was inspired to create the watch after seeing the movie *2001: A Space Odyssey*. On 4 April 1972, the Pulsar was produced and marketed. It sold for a phenomenal price ($2,100 US) and was made using 18-carat gold. The watch had a red light-emitting diode display. Most people couldn't afford a digital watch but Texas Instruments started to mass produce them, replacing the gold surround with much cheaper plastic. In America the watches retailed for $20 in 1975 but were reduced to $10. Pulsar went on to lose $6 million and the brand was sold to Seiko.

In 1975 Sinclair Research sold their own version called The Black Watch in the UK. These continued to be sold for several years, but problems with production and returned faulty watches led the company to stop manufacturing them. However, for a while they were the must-have item and towards the end of the 1970s, everyone had one. The technology greatly improved in the 1980s.

On 19 November 1970 the floppy disk was invented to store information when computers first appeared on the market. However, the internet was a long way off and by the time every home owned its own computer, floppy disks were already becoming redundant as more information had to be stored. They were replaced by CDs and then by DVDs.

On 1 July 1971 email was invented. American Computer programmer Ray Tomlinson was the sender of the first email (to himself on another computer) on the ARPANET (Advanced Research Projects Agency Network). The network initially just connected universities, but would later lead to the introduction of the internet. However, in the early 1970s, with no internet, hardly anyone was able to send an email. Its appeal would only gain momentum after 1989 with internet enabled home computers and the invention of the World Wide Web by British scientist Tim Berners-Lee.

On 26 August 1971 Liquid Crystal Display was invented. Amazingly, LCD had been around for some time before we all got flat-screen televisions. Back in the 1970s, presenters on the BBC science programme, Tomorrow's World, suggested that by using the technology we would one day have flat televisions that we could hang on our walls. It took technology almost another forty years before this was possible and today, it's very hard to find a home that still has a bulky last-century television, complete with a tube. Today LCDs are used in a wide range of other products including computer monitors, instrument panels, aircraft cockpit displays and bus direction displays, as well as on indoor and outdoor signposts. Smaller LCD screens are found in portable devices such as digital cameras, watches, calculators, mobile telephones as well as smartphones.

Pong, the first home video game, which plugged straight into the aerial socket of the television set. It came with various games including tennis and squash but all were much the same, featuring two bats and a ball.

The CT scanner was invented in 1972. Nobel Prize winner Sir Godfrey Hounsfield invented the first commercially viable CT scanner at the EMI Central Research Laboratories in Hayes using X-rays incorporating computerized tomography, an idea which he had first conceived in 1967. On 1 October 1971 the first EMI-Scanner, which was installed in Atkinson Morley Hospital in Wimbledon, performed the first brain scan of a patient.

On 16 June 1972 Pong, the first home video game was invented. Pong was a two-dimensional table tennis game which could be played at home on the television. Previously such games had only appeared in arcades. At the time the gaming machine, created by Atari, contained the highest performing microchip of its time. By the mid-1970s, Pong became the must-have game for home entertainment and spawned many successors including Nintendo's Coleco game console in the early 1980s. Amazingly, the basic bat and ball game, led on to the weird and wonderful highly advanced home video games that we have today.

In the 1970s cassette decks were introduced in cars, as were the more bulky cartridge players, meaning that you could take your music wherever you wanted. Many cars also had basic radios. In the later 1970s CB radio, a craze from America, hit the UK and many people had them fitted to their cars so that they could have free conversations with other road users. The first electric cars were on the roads by the

A National Panasonic cassette player. Portable players came out in the early 1970s and proved very popular with teenagers.

1970s. In 1966 a factory on the Isle of Wight built 100 cars, the Enfield 8000, which arose after the United Kingdom Electricity Council ran a competition to produce a car which ran entirely on electricity. The idea didn't catch on and production of the car was halted in 1976.

On 12 February 1973 it was discovered that genetic engineering was possible. Today, we're still struggling with the concept but, hopefully, one day soon, all our ills will be cured.

On 23 April 1973 the barcode was created. Today, there isn't an item that doesn't come with a barcode, including identification bracelets for newborn babies. In June 1974 the first scannable barcode appeared on a pack of Wrigley's chewing gum. Even in the UK in the 1970s, they were unheard of and didn't really take off until the 1980s.

On 23 October 1973 the disposable lighter was invented. It was handy for smokers who didn't want to buy matches or carry a heavy normal lighter. Today, they're still around and are the scourge of every beach up and down the country.

Also in 1973, an early touch-screen was developed at CERN although the technology didn't reach most people until the twenty-first century.

Between 1973 and 1975 the internet protocol suite was developed for the Defense Advanced Research Projects Agency by Vinton Cerf and Robert E. Kahn. This created the basis for the modern internet although, for most of us, it was a long time coming.

On 30 November 1974 the Post-It note was invented. Post-It notes proved invaluable for people taking notes from the phone or leaving messages on the fridge or elsewhere for family and friends. Again, they arrived in the UK much later but were commonplace in the 1980s.

In 1975 Eastman Kodak and Steve Sasson constructed the first digital camera. Made from other pieced-together camera parts, it weighed a bulky 8lbs. It was another twenty years before the technology really took off. Today, it's very rare for anyone to use film.

On 30 March 1975 the push-through top on drinks cans was invented. Cans of fizzy drinks all have push-through tops nowadays. In the 1970s and beyond, all drink tins had ring pulls and the push-through top is still quite recent.

In 1977 Voyager 1 and Voyager 2 were launched into space to collect data on Jupiter, Saturn, Uranus, Neptune and the solar system.

On 18 October 1976 the ink-jet printer was invented and was in use long before people owned their first home computer. By the 1990s owning an ink jet along with a scanner and a computer became essential for many people.

Voyager 1 and Voyager 2 were launched into space by NASA in September 1977. The space probes collected valuable data on Jupiter, Saturn, Uranus and Neptune and sent back outstanding photos of the planets. During August 2012 Voyager 1 left the solar system and entered interstellar space. In case they encounter alien life, both craft carry information about our planet on a Golden Record imprinted with spoken greetings in fifty-five languages and sounds and images chosen to portray the diversity of life on Earth.

In 1977 the Apple II computer was released. Primarily developed by Steve Wozniak with the entrepreneur Steve Jobs, the machine led to Apple's later overwhelming involvement within the computer industry and other markets.

Also in 1977 the Commodore PET (Personal Electronic Transactor) was released. It became a best seller in Canadian and American markets. It paved the way for the later popular home computer, the Commodore 64. The 8-bit home computer was introduced in January 1982 and over 17 million were sold to consumers.

On 25 December 1977 the MRI scanner was invented. Magnetic Resonance Imaging allowed doctors and surgeons, for the first time, to obtain detailed images of the inside of the body.

On 30 March 1978 the Jarvik-7 artificial heart was invented by Robert Jarvik. It was implanted in patient Barney Clark, a dentist, in 1982 and the operation caught the attention of media around the world. Clark died 112 days later.

The Sony Walkman was developed in Japan by engineer Nobutoshi Kihara before being introduced on to the market in 1979. The portable players proved hugely popular.

On 25 July 1978 Louise Brown was born at Oldham General Hospital, Greater Manchester and became the world's first baby to be conceived by IVF (In Vitro Fertilization).

Nowadays, i-Pods and MP3 players are commonplace, but the first personal music player appeared on the market in the late 1970s. The Sony Walkman allowed people, for the first time, to listen to music while on the move.

In 1978 a prototype was built in Japan by engineer Nobutoshi Kihara for the Sony co-founder, Masaru Ibuka. Ibuka wanted to be able to listen to music while on long plane journeys so suggested the idea to Kihara. This eventually led to the first Walkmans being sold in Japan in 1979, shortly afterwards being available all over the world. When the players first came out, anyone wearing one outdoors would have been a source of conversation, but they soon became commonplace.

Televisions also changed much over the decade. They went from basic push-button or dial black-and-white sets to larger, clearer, colour sets, although remote controls were still unheard of in the UK. Technology changed greatly over the 1970s. Many of the inventions of the decade led on to much of the equipment that we use today.

Celebrity quotes:

'*When I first looked back at the Earth, standing on the Moon, I cried.*' Alan Shepard talking about the Apollo 14 mission in 1971.

'*Imagination will often carry us to worlds that never were. But without it we go nowhere.*' Carl Sagan.

'*I think it's fair to say that personal computers have become the most empowering tool we've ever created. They're tools of communication, they're tools of creativity, and they can be shaped by their user.*' Bill Gates.

'*Being the richest man in the cemetery doesn't matter to me. Going to bed at night saying you've done something wonderful, that's what matters to me.*' Steve Jobs.

'*It is only when they go wrong that machines remind you how powerful they are.*' Clive James.

Chapter 9

Transport

At the beginning of the 1970s, many people still didn't own their own cars. Cars were a luxury and it was very unusual for a family to have more than one. Many streets were free of vehicles allowing children to play football and other games in the road.

Double-decker buses were used by most people going to work or into town for shopping. At the time, buses still had smartly dressed conductors who came and collected your fare once you'd sat down before issuing a ticket from a huge paper roll in a portable dispensing machine.

Cars and petrol were expensive at the time (petrol was five shillings a gallon) and many people paid for their first cars by hire purchase. Most bought second-hand cars with only the well-off buying brand new models. Most new car owners had some knowledge of how to fix their cars as they were quite often unreliable and broke down. Older cars were prone to overheating, proved difficult to start on cold or wet days, while, eventually, they also suffered from rust. A knowledge of car DIY was essential and although the AA and RAC existed, most people weren't members.

The top ten best selling cars of the 1970s were the Ford Cortina, the Ford Escort, the Mini, the Morris Marina, the Vauxhall Viva, the Austin/Morris 1100/1300, the Austin Allegro, the Ford Capri, the Hillman Avenger and the Austin Maxi.

In 1972 Ford released the Cortina Mk3 which featured more up-to-date styling. The Cortina GXL interior was more modern and American in appearance, complete with chrome trim. The car came in several models including L (basic), XL (more luxury), GT (sports), GXL (more luxurious) and the top of the range 2000E. The GXL

A Ford Cortina, one of Britain's favourite cars of the 1970s.

offered wood trim, velour seats together with a chrome trimmed black vinyl roof.

In 1976, the Ford Cortina Mk III was replaced by the Mk IV, a car more sober in appearance. In 1979, the Mk V was introduced. The car was eventually phased out in 1982 to make way for the Sierra.

Ford Escorts were incredibly popular during the 1970s with the company selling over one million cars in the decade. The Escort had been introduced in 1967 as a replacement for the Ford Anglia. It had a stylish body and also came in a range of models including saloons, sports and luxury versions. By 1975 the Escort had a more squared-off body, complete with what were then modern square headlamps. By 1979 there was a range of models including the 1100, 1300, 1600, 1800 and 2000cc. By 1980 the Mk III was released, ready for a new decade.

The Mini was eleven years old by the start of the decade but was still hugely popular with drivers. Economical, nippy and easy to park, in the 1970s, it was still one of Britain's favourite cars. British Leyland decided to drop the Austin and Morris brand and just called the car the Mini. The basic range included the Mini 850 and Mini 1000 featuring small 850cc and 1000cc engines. The Clubman was a more squared-off version and the estate featured fake wooden panels. A sporty 1275

King's Road in London in the 1970s featuring many classic cars of the decade. On the right of the picture is the popular Renault 5.

GT was also available. The shape of the car remained much the same throughout the 1970s.

The Morris Marina was released as a replacement for the Morris Minor. It was produced to rival the Ford Escort and was styled by Roy Haynes who had previously worked for Ford. The two-door version was meant to appeal to the under 40s. The car never reached the sales of the Escort but was still the fourth bestselling car of the 1970s.

The Vauxhall Viva was very similar to many Ford models, even down to the colour. The Viva had first been manufactured in 1963 and was revised in 1970. The new Viva was stylish and similar to the Ford Escort. The basic model was the HC but it also came with a range of engine sizes and other options with the sporty Firenza SL being the top of the range. The Viva disappeared in 1979.

The Austin/Morris 1100/1300 had sold well in the 1960s and continued to sell well into the early 1970s. It came in 1970s colours including purple and orange and proved spacious and reliable. A sports model was available, the Austin 1300GT, which came complete

A Ford Capri. The car was famously featured in the popular television show The Professionals which starred Lewis Collins and Martin Shaw as Bodie and Doyle.

with a black vinyl roof. British Leyland replaced the car with the Allegro in 1973.

The Austin Allegro was the seventh best-selling car of the 1970s but it lacked the style of some of the Ford models. The Vanden Plas 1500 came with a range of engine sizes from 1100cc to 1750cc and included real wood facia and leather seats; picnic tables were also included but proved unpopular with buyers. The lack of sales (approximately 65,000 a year) contributed to British Leyland's downfall in 1975. Austin-Rover dropped the Allegro in 1982 and it was superseded by the Maestro.

The Ford Capri was a sportier version of the Escort. It was launched in 1969 and sold in large numbers throughout the 1970s. At the top of the range was the 3000E which was capable of a top speed of 122 mph and could go from 0-60 mph in eight seconds. The car also featured reclining seats, a clock and a push-button radio, all very modern at the time. The steering wheel and gear knob came complete with simulated leather, seen as luxurious at the time.

A Hillman Avenger. The car was introduced in 1970 and competed for sales with the Ford Escort and Vauxhall Viva. It was a popular family car and was eventually updated in 1976 before becoming the Chrysler Avenger.

The Hillman Avenger was launched in 1970 and was accompanied by television adverts showing the car being offloaded from an aeroplane while the theme from the popular television series The Avengers played in the background. Stylish and modern, the car was smaller than the Hillman Hunter and its main competition came from the Escort and the Viva. It sold well and was updated before becoming the Chrysler Avenger in 1976.

The tenth most popular car of the 1970s was the Austin Maxi. It was one of the first cars to feature a hatchback and also came with a five-speed gearbox. It was never as popular as it should have been mainly because the public didn't like the design, the gearbox didn't perform well and the 1500cc engine wasn't powerful enough. In 1971 it was updated with a new grill, wood finish fascia and a more powerful 1750cc engine. Although the car didn't sell in great numbers, people liked the ease of the hatchback and this was adopted by many future models.

The police drove a variety of cars in the 1970s. At the beginning of the 1970s these were mainly Austin 1100s (Panda cars) and later Ford Escorts (known as 'a jam sandwich').

Picadilly Street, London in the late 1970s complete with black taxi cabs and red double-decker buses. The cinema in the background is showing *Confessions of a Driving Instructor*.

Ice cream vans visited housing estates often and were a regular site on the streets of the UK. Their distinct chimes (often 'Greensleeves', 'Popeye the Sailorman' or 'Raindrops Keep Falling on my Head') brought children running out of their houses to buy an ice cream or lolly.

Petrol stations did their best to attract customers. Many offered free gifts such as glass tumblers, World Cup coins, Green Shield Stamps and a whole variety of different gifts. Many garages were not self-service at the beginning of the decade and a man would come out on to the forecourt to fill up your car as well as, sometimes, checking the oil, wiping the windscreen and topping up the radiator. Popular garages included Esso, Shell, National and Mobil.

The 1973 oil crisis led to fuel shortages in the UK. By 1974 there were long queues at garages and fights sometimes broke out. In some areas, the police were called in to keep order.

The James Bond movie *The Spy Who Loved Me* (1977), starring Roger Moore, featured a very desirable car at the time, the Lotus Esprit.

Starsky and Hutch's Gran Torino. The car featured on the show every week and became one of the best remembered television cars of the decade.

The Lotus in the film was not only a superfast and classy sports car but also, memorably, an underwater submarine. No real Lotus Esprit of the time would have fared well under water. Some film and tv shows became known for their cars. The Persuaders (1971), starring Roger Moore and Tony Curtis, featured the Ferrari Dino 246 GT (driven by Danny Wilde) and the Aston Martin DBS (driven by Brett Sinclair). The Sweeney (1975-1978) featured the Consul 3000 GT in the first three series and the Mk2 Granada 2.8iS in the last series while The Professionals (1977-1983) featured a Rover P6 2000 Automatic (driven by both Bodie and Doyle), Rover 3500 SD1 (driven by Cowley), a Triumph TR7 (driven by Doyle), a Triumph Dolomite Sprint (driven by Bodie and Doyle) and a Ford Granada Mk II 2.0 L (driven by Cowley) as well as many others. However, the car best remembered from the show was the Ford Capri, driven by both characters, which led later on, to much interest in the model.

Starsky and Hutch featured a Gran Torino in red with a white stripe, The Dukes of Hazzard (1979) drove a Dodge Charger named The General Lee, Jim Rockford in The Rockford Files (1974) drove a Gold Pontiac Firebird and Kojak drove a bronze 1973 Buick Century Regal 455 – all cars which looked fantastic on the television but were unheard of on the streets of Great Britain at the time.

Cars on Kensington High Street in 1976. As well as classic cars, such as the Mini, fashions of the day can be seen including vest tops and flares.

Other traffic on the roads included milk-delivery vans which ran on electric batteries and were only capable of very slow speeds, works vans (although not in the quantity you see today), delivery lorries and motor bikes. Motor scooters had become very popular with young people in the 60s, especially 'Mods' and this continued in the early part of the decade with Vespa and Lambretta, the preferred makes.

The television programme Top Gear was first shown on BBC Midlands in 1977 and was originally presented by Angela Rippon and Tom Coyne. The main BBC network picked up the programme and it was first shown on BBC2 on 13 July 1978. The weekly 30-minute programme continued to be hosted by Angela Rippon with co-host Barrie Gill. Every week Noel Edmonds tested new cars and, in 1980, he became the main presenter.

As the 1970s moved on, more and more people owned their own cars. There was more disposable income but, even so, most still bought second-hand models.

In more advanced transport, NASA sent further Apollo missions to the Moon in the 1970s. The Apollo 13 mission had to return to Earth due to a malfunction during April 1970. However, Apollo 14 (January 1971), Apollo 15 (July 1971), Apollo 16 (April 1972) and Apollo 17 (December 1972) landed another twelve astronauts on the Moon

A Rolls Royce with the rare numberplate RR1, together with other classic vehicles of the decade feature in this photo.

before the programme finally ended. Amazingly, by 1972, people had apparently grown tired of watching men walking on the Moon. Apollo 18 and 19 were cancelled due to budget cuts. Altogether, there were just twelve men who had actually walked on the Moon with another six who had travelled to the Moon but had remained in the Lunar Module. The first man to walk on the Moon was Neil Armstrong on 21 July 1969 and the last was Gene Cernan in December 1972. There were many plans to return but no one has set foot on the Moon since that date.

The cars of the 1970s were both stylish and classic although they could be unreliable and prone to rust. However, they remain some of the most iconic vehicles of the last fifty years.

Celebrity quotes:

'*A lot of people criticize Formula 1 as an unnecessary risk. But what would life be like if we only did what is necessary?*' Niki Lauda.

'*The car is a character in the piece – I've never liked the car, I submitted to its objectionable popularity.*' Paul Michael Glaser.

'After Apollo 17, America stopped looking towards the next horizon. The United States had become a space-faring nation, but threw it away. We have sacrificed space exploration for space exploitation, which is interesting but scarcely visionary.' Eugene Cernan.

'If God had meant for us to walk, why did he give us feet that fit car pedals?' Stirling Moss.

'I hate the standard of stupid and selfish driving we have in this country. We are the worst I've come across.' Martin Shaw.

'Anybody can jump a motorcycle. The trouble begins when you try to land it.' Evel Knievel.

Celebrity Memory: Paul Martin (Flog It!)

I recall the great music of the 1970s with my favourites being David Bowie and T Rex. On television, I enjoyed The Six Million Dollar Man, The Incredible Hulk, Top of the Pops, The Two Ronnies, The Generation Game and Morecambe and Wise. In sport, I remember the World Cup and England's part in all of them. England were the reigning World Cup champions in 1970 but were beaten in the quarter finals in 1970 with Brazil winning the title. In 1974 West Germany won the cup and in 1978 the cup was won by Argentina.

My family moved to Cornwall in the 1970s and I remember growing up on the beach and the long, hot summer of 1976.

In fashions, I recall flares! Everyone had flares together with long hair, tank tops and flared long sleeve T-shirts.

Of the whacky decor, I remember Mary Quant bedheads, teak furniture, Whitefriars glass everywhere and white TV sets.

The era had many new gadgets during the 1970s and I recall fondly the Sony Walkman, the waffle and the toasted sandwich maker and colour TV.

In transport, I remember hopping on and off London double-decker buses, jumping off before it stopped and hanging on to the pole, as well as individual carriages on trains and upholstered spring seats. Trains were never full and four times longer. Those were the days for travel!

Chapter 10

Notable Highlights

1970

On 31 March a 17-year-old Dana won the Eurovision Song Contest for Ireland with the song 'All Kinds of Everything'. The contest took place in Amsterdam. Mary Hopkin, singing for England, came second with 'Knock, Knock Who's There?'.

Paul McCartney announced that he was leaving the Beatles on 10 April which signalled the end of the band. John Lennon had already decided to leave.

The computer floppy disk was introduced. With the later introduction of recordable CDs, and later DVDs, floppy disks slowly disappeared and are now rarely used.

'Your Song' from Elton John's second album (entitled Elton John) made it into the Top Ten in both the UK and the US making it his first hit single. In America it was originally released as the B-side to 'Take Me to the Pilot'.

During April Apollo 13 was launched on its way to the moon. On board were astronauts James A. Lovell, John L. Swigert and Fred W. Haise. The launch date was 11 April but the mission had to be aborted due to oxygen failure and the crew returned safely to Earth on 17 April.

In May the Beatles released their final album 'Let It Be'. The album went to number one all around the world with 'The Long and Winding Road' topping the charts in the US. The album also featured 'Across the Universe' and 'Get Back'.

On Monday 4 May the Ohio National Guard shot several unarmed college students protesting against the Cambodian campaign at the Kent State University. Four were killed and nine wounded.

Brazil's 1970 World Cup team featuring Pelé. They beat Italy 4-1 to win the championship.

Edward Heath became the Prime Minister of Great Britain on 18 June defeating Harold Wilson. He had been elected leader of the Conservative Party in 1965 and remained in power until March 1974.

In football, during June, Brazil won the World Cup in Mexico by beating Italy 4–1. England were beaten by West Germany in the quarter finals. The England team included many players from the 1966 winning team including Bobby Moore, Geoff Hurst, Gordon Banks, Bobby Charlton, Jackie Charlton and Nobby Stiles.

On 21 July the Aswan High Dam was completed. The dam was built between 1960 and 1970 and stopped the Nile Valley flooding every year. This had a major effect on the economy and culture of Egypt.

The statue of Ramses the Great at the Great Temple of Abu Simbel being reassembled. It was moved during the building of the Aswan High Dam.

The Isle of Wight Festival, featuring Jimi Hendrix, the Doors, Joan Baez, Jethro Tull, the Who and Chicago, took place in August. Also playing were the Moody Blues, Miles Davis, Joni Mitchell and Free. Over 600,000 people attended the festival.

During September four jet airliners on their way to New York City and London were hijacked by members of the Popular Front for the Liberation of Palestine (PFLP). They were forced to land at Dawson's Field, an airstrip near Zarka, Jordan. A fifth hijacked passenger plane joined them soon after. The 310 hostages were later rescued and one hijacker was killed.

On 18 September Jimi Hendrix died from a suspected barbiturates overdose. He was found unconscious at the flat of Monika Dannemann at the Samarkand Hotel at 22 Lansdowne Crescent, Notting Hill in London. He was taken to St Mary Abbot's Hospital but never recovered.

Janis Joplin who died of a drugs overdose in October 1970. Her biggest hit was 'Piece of My Heart' which was released in 1968.

The unmanned Luna 16 spacecraft landed on the Moon on 20 September and collected samples from the surface before lifting off the next day. It was part of the Soviet Luna programme and was the first robotic probe to land on the Moon's surface.

On 4 October, Janis Joplin was found dead in her room at the Landmark Motor Hotel in Hollywood. She had died of a heroin overdose aged just 27.

President Nixon announced the withdrawal of 40,000 American troops from Vietnam on 12 October. Soon afterwards South Vietnamese troops carried out a new offensive in Cambodia.

1971

The Apollo 14 mission lifted off on 31 January and became the third successful manned landing on the Moon. On board were astronauts

Alan B. Shepard, Edgar D. Mitchell and Stuart A. Roosa who touched down on the surface on 5 February. Shepard famously played golf on the Moon. They returned to Earth on 9 February.

On 15 February Decimalisation Day took place and the UK and Northern Ireland both switched over to decimal currency. Items were priced with both pre-decimal and decimal prices (e.g. 1s/5p) for many years until people got used to the new system. A huge publicity campaign promoted and explained the new money.

The rebuilding of London Bridge, which had originally spanned the Thames before being sold and transported to the US, was completed in Arizona. It was originally built in the 1830s and was dismantled and shipped to America in 1967.

Evel Knievel set a new world record by jumping over nineteen cars on a motor cycle on 28 February. On his Harley-Davidson XR-750, he completed the jump at the Ontario Motor Speedway in Ontario, California. The event was filmed so that it could be included in a movie about Knieval which starred George Hamilton.

VCRs were introduced although most families didn't own one for at least another ten years. The first machines used the Sony U-matic format.

On 7 March the postal workers' strike, which was led by UPW General secretary Tom Jackson, ended after forty-seven days. It was Britain's first national postal strike. Workers had demanded a pay rise of 15-20 per cent and went on strike when a lower offer was put to them.

On 8 March Muhammad Ali was defeated by Joe Frazier at Madison Square Garden. The match became known as 'The Fight of the Century'.

During April, over 500,000 people in Washington protested against the Vietnam War. There were 12,000 arrests for engaging in mass civil disobedience.

On 9 May Arsenal won the FA cup. They beat Liverpool 2-1 after extra time. Steve Heighway scored for Liverpool with Arsenal's goals being scored by Eddie Kelly and Charlie George, in extra time.

A leaky valve on board the Russian Soyuz 11 spacecraft led to the death of the crew after their air supply was lost. The capsule

James Irwin on the moon on 1 August 1971 as part of the Apollo 15 mission. The astronauts returned successfully to Earth a few days later on 7 August 1971.

depressurised as the crew were making plans for re-entry. To date, the three astronauts of Soyuz 11 are the only humans to have died in space.

On 3 July the Doors lead singer, Jim Morrison, was found dead in his bath in Paris. He was 27 and the cause of death was recorded as 'heart failure.'

The Apollo 15 mission to the Moon was launched on 26 July and successfully landed on 30 July. On the following day, David Scott and James Irwin became the first astronauts to use the lunar rover. They returned to Earth on 7 August.

In the autumn the first pocket calculator was introduced in the US. Although highly expensive, their cost was greatly reduced once they were mass produced.

A bomb exploded in the Post Office Tower in London on 31 October. The IRA later claimed responsibility. The tower and restaurant closed to the public shortly afterwards.

1972

After fourteen unarmed marchers were killed in Derry, Northern Ireland, Sunday 30 January became known as 'Bloody Sunday'. Altogether twenty-six protesters were shot in the Bogside area of Derry.

On 2 March the Pioneer 10 spacecraft was launched at Cape Kennedy and became the first man-made satellite to leave the solar system. Contact was lost with the spacecraft on 23 January 2003 with a loss of electrical power to its transmitter. By then, it had travelled 12 billion kilometres.

On 4 April the first Pulsar digital watch was released. It was made in 18-carat gold and sold for $2,100. It came with a red light-emitting diode (LED) display. Digital watches were later mass produced and were greatly reduced in price.

The Summer Olympics were held in Munich between 26 August and 11 September. They were marred by the murder of eleven Israeli athletes by the Arab terrorist group Black September on 5 September.

Mark Spitz won seven gold medals at the Summer Olympics in Munich. He retired from competition soon after although he was only 22 years old at the time. Spitz later worked for ABC Sports and covered the 1976 Summer Olympics in Montreal.

On 10 September Emerson Fittipaldi became the youngest Formula One World Champion at 25 years old. In 1974 he left Lotus and drove for McLaren with whom he won the title once more.

On 17 September M*A*S*H premiered on US television. It starred Alan Alda and Wayne Rogers as army medics during the Korean War. The show proved hugely popular and continued until 28 February 1983.

The cast of the popular US comedy, M*A*S*H which starred Alan Alda, Wayne Rogers, Loretta Swit, Larry Linville, Gary Burghoff and McLean Stevenson.

Pong, Atari's first commercial video game, was released on 29 November and became hugely successful. Home consoles sold worldwide.

The last manned Moon mission, Apollo 17, took off on 7 December. On board were astronauts Eugene Cernan, Ronald Evans and Harrison Schmitt. They successfully landed on 11 December and Eugene Cernan became the last man to walk on the Moon on 14 December.

1973

The UK, the Republic of Ireland and Denmark entered the European Economic Community, which would later become the European Union on 1 January.

On 4 January the BBC first showed The Last of the Summer Wine which continued until August 2010. The programme originally starred Peter Sallis, Michael Bates and Bill Owen.

Skylab was America's first space station and orbited the Earth between 1973 and 1979. The photo was the last crew to leave the station.

On 14 January Elvis Presley's live concert 'Aloha from Hawaii' was watched by more people than those who had watched the Moon landings. The show was broadcast by satellite and aired in over forty countries.

President Richard Nixon announced the end of offensive action in North Vietnam on 15 January, following peace talks in Paris. However, air assaults continued against communist forces in South Vietnam, Laos and Cambodia.

On 22 January Joe Frazier was defeated by George Foreman winning him the heavyweight world boxing championship. The fight was billed as 'The Sunshine Showdown'.

With the signing of the Paris Peace Accords, the Vietnam War ended on 27 January. US troops began to withdraw shortly afterwards.

Tottenham Hotspur won the football league cup at Wembley by beating Norwich City on 3 March. The final score was 1-0 and the goal was scored by Ralph Coates.

On 17 March Pink Floyd released their album, 'Dark Side of the Moon'. It was the eighth LP from the group and went on to sell 45 million copies. Two singles were released from the album, 'Money' and 'Us and Them'.

Sunderland won the FA Cup final on 5 May. They beat Leeds United with the final score being 1-0. Ian Porterfield scored the winning goal.

On 14 May Skylab was launched becoming the America's first space station. It orbited Earth between 1973 and 1979 and included a workshop and solar observatory.

On 10 July John Paul Getty III was kidnapped in the Piazza Farnese in Rome. He was later released after a ransom of $2.9 million was paid. However, by this time, the kidnappers had cut off his ear. The kidnappers were later caught although most of the ransom money was never recovered.

President Nixon announced, 'I am not a crook!' to 400 Associated Press editors on 17 November in the midst of the Watergate scandal.

1974

The crew of Skylab returned to Earth on 8 February after a record eighty-four days in space. The final crew included Gerald Carr, Edward Gibson and William Pogue.

On 10 March Hiroo Onoda, a Second World War Japanese officer, finally surrendered in the Philippines. His former commander personally relieved him from his duty after travelling from Japan.

The Terracotta Army of China's first emperor, Qin Shi Huang, dating from 210 BC was discovered in Xi'an in China.

On 6 April, the Eurovision song contest was won by Sweden with the song 'Waterloo' performed by ABBA. The competition was held in Brighton. The British entry was 'Long Live Love' sung by Olivia Newton-John which came fourth.

Hiroo Onoda, the last Japanese soldier to surrender after the end of the Second World War.

The FIFA World Cup was won by West Germany on 7 July after they beat the Netherlands 2-1 in the final. England failed to qualify and Sir Alf Ramsey resigned as manager soon after.

Due to the Watergate scandal, President Richard Nixon offered his resignation on 8 August. Gerald Ford became the new President of the US on the following day.

On 23 September, the BBC launched Ceefax. The information service ended on 23 October 2012 due to the digital switch over.

Muhammad Ali knocked out George Foreman in the eighth round in Zaire and became heavyweight world champion on 30 October. The match became known as the 'Rumble in the Jungle'.

1975

Work on the British end of the Channel Tunnel was abandoned on 1 January. The Labour Party cancelled the project due to rising costs and the uncertainty about its EEC membership.

On 11 February Margaret Thatcher became the new leader of the Conservative Party after defeating Edward Heath.

On 1 March Aston Villa won the Football League Cup. Aston Villa beat Norwich City 1-0. The match was played at Wembley Stadium.

Richard Nixon who resigned
as President of the USA
during August 1974 due to the
Watergate scandal.

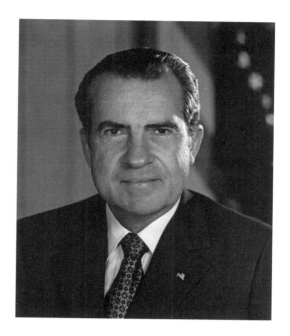

On 4 March Charlie Chaplin was knighted by the Queen. He was accompanied to the ceremony at Buckingham Palace by his fourth wife, Oona, and the two youngest of his nine children.

Teach-In, a band from the Netherlands, won the Eurovision Song Contest with the song, 'Ding-a-dong' on 22 March. The event took place in Stockholm, Sweden. England came ninth with 'Let Me Be the One' by The Shadows.

On 4 April Bill Gates and Paul Allen founded Microsoft. The company went on to become the most dominating force in the computer world and Microsoft Windows is used on most systems.

On 19 June Lord Lucan was found guilty, in his absence, of the murder of his nanny Sandra Rivett. The nanny had been found bludgeoned to death in the basement of the Lucan family home on 7 November 1974.

On 17 July the America's Apollo and Russia's Soyuz spacecraft docked in orbit for the first time. The Apollo crew included Thomas P. Stafford, Vance D. Brand and Donald K. Slayton. On board the Soyuz were Alexey Leonov and Valeri Kubasov.

On 1 October Muhammad Ali beat Joe Frazier in Manila to become the heavyweight champion of the world. The fight became known as the 'Thriller in Manila'.

On 27 November, Ross McWhirter, the co-founder of the Guinness Book of Records, was shot dead by the IRA. He had previously offered a reward of £50,000 for information leading to the conviction of the people responsible for the recent spate of bombings in England.

1976

On 21 January Concorde made its first commercial flight. It continued to fly until 2003 after the crash of Air France Flight 4590, which resulted in the deaths of all passengers and crew.

On 29 January twelve IRA bombs exploded in the West End of London. The bombings were the first in central London for over a year.

On 16 March Harold Wilson resigned as Prime Minister. He claimed that he was physically and mentally exhausted and had always planned on resigning once he reached 60 years old.

Patty Hearst became famous world-wide after being found guilty of robbing a San Francisco bank. She was sent to prison for seven years. William Horsley Orrick Jr. who sentenced her, stated, 'rebellious young people who, for whatever reason become revolutionaries, and voluntarily commit criminal acts will be punished.'

On 3 April Brotherhood of Man won the Eurovision Song Contest for Britain with 'Save Your Kisses For Me'. The contest took place in The Hague, Netherlands. Four countries tied for first place in the Eurovision song contest in 1969 making that the last UK win before 1974.

On 5 April James Callaghan became the new Prime Minister of Great Britain after Harold Wilson's resignation. He remained in the position until 4 May 1979 when Margaret Thatcher won the General Election.

The Cod War ended on 1 June after an agreement between Iceland and the UK. The UK agreed to a 200-nautical-mile Icelandic exclusive fishery zone which proved a poor deal for British fishermen.

Johnny Rotten and The Sex Pistols. The outrageous group was banned by many television and radio stations at the time.

The year had one of the longest, hottest summers. The heatwave reached its peak in July whilst drought conditions continued. Standpipes were set up in some areas.

Israeli commandos rescued 103 Air France hostages at Entebbe on 4 July. All of the hijackers as well as three hostages and forty-five Ugandan soldiers were killed.

On 17 July the Summer Olympics began in Montreal. Great Britain finished thirteenth in the medal rankings achieving three gold medals, five silver and five bronze.

Big Ben stopped working on 5 August and didn't run for the next nine months. The problem was blamed on metal fatigue which caused a fracture in the chiming mechanism.

On 3 September the Viking 2 spacecraft landed on Mars. It continued to operate on the surface of the planet for 1316 days before being finally turned off on 11 April 1980 when its batteries stopped working.

The band U2 were formed on 25 September, after drummer Larry Mullen Jr requested members for a new band at his Dublin school.

The Sex Pistols gave their now-famous four-lettered word interview on the Bill Grundy Show on 1 December.

1977

Jimmy Carter became the 39th President of the United States on 20 January. He succeeded Gerald Ford and stayed in the position until 20 January 1981.

On 27 January the Sex Pistols were sacked from their EMI record label. They were later signed to Richard Branson's Virgin Records.

On 4 February Fleetwood Mac released the album, 'Rumours'. It became their most successful release and sold over 45 million copies worldwide.

On 8 April the Clash's debut album was released. It reached number twelve in the UK charts and was described as one of the greatest punk albums of all time.

The M5 motorway was completed on 1 May when the Exminster section was declared open by the Prime Minister James Callaghan.

On 17 May Queen Elizabeth II began her Silver Jubilee tour at Glasgow. Throughout the summer, she travelled the whole of the UK.

On 21 May Manchester United won the FA Cup. They beat Liverpool 2-1. The goals were scored by Stuart Pearson and Jimmy Greenhoff for Manchester and Jimmy Case for Liverpool.

Liverpool won the European Cup on 25 May. Liverpool beat Borussia Mönchengladbach 3-1. The final took place at the Stadio Olimpico in Rome.

On 25 May *Star Wars* opened in the US. It was first shown in the UK on 27 December. It went on to become one of the most successful movies of all time.

Silver Jubilee celebrations were held around the UK between 6 and 9 June. Street parties, accompanied by much flag waving, were held in every town and city.

On 10 August, Kenny Dalglish became Britain's most expensive footballer after a £444,000 transfer. The fee was paid by Liverpool's manager, Bob Paisley. Dalglish began his career with Celtic in 1971.

The Space Shuttle made its first test flight on 12 August. Operational flights began in 1982 and it was retired from service on 21 July 2011.

Elvis Presley, the king of rock and roll, died aged 42 at his home in Memphis on 16 August. There was an outpouring of grief from fans and admirers all around the world.

Marc Bolan died in a car crash after his mini hit a tree on 16 September. The mourners at his funeral included David Bowie, Rod Stewart, Tony Visconti and Steve Harley. One of the floral tributes at the service was in the shape of a swan in recognition of his hit single 'Ride a White Swan'.

Freddie Laker launched his budget airline, 'Skytrain' on 26 September. By 1982 the company had gone bankrupt owing a total of £250 million.

On 14 October, Bing Crosby died while playing golf at the La Moraleja Golf Course near Madrid.

Saturday Night Fever was released on 14 December. It starred John Travolta as Anthony 'Tony' Manero and Karen Lynn Gorney as Stephanie Mangano. The film became a huge hit partly down to the memorable Bee Gees soundtrack.

Charlie Chaplin died on 25 December. Chaplin was buried at the Corsier-sur-Vevey cemetery. On 1 March 1978 his body was stolen and held for ransom but was later recovered and re-interred in the Corsier cemetery.

1978

On 14 January the Sex Pistols played their final show. The concert took place in San Francisco. Johnny Rotten finished the performance with the words, 'Ever get the feeling you've been cheated? Good night.'

On 16 January fire fighters ended their strike which had continued for three months. Fire crews decided to accept a pay rise of 10 per cent together with reduced working hours.

Anna Ford became the first female newsreader on ITN on 13 February. She later helped launch TV-am, the first British breakfast television programme in 1983.

On 21 June, *Evita* opened in London. The musical was written by Andrew Lloyd Webber and Tim Rice. Elaine Paige played the lead role on stage but Julie Covington sang on the LP record, released in 1976, which produced the hit 'Don't Cry For Me, Argentina'.

On 25 July, Louise Brown became the first test-tube baby. The IVF proceedure was developed by Patrick Steptoe and Robert Edwards. Her younger sister, Natalie, was also conceived by IVF four years later.

Bakeries rationed bread on 4 November after a nationwide bakers strike. The strike led to panic buying.

The Eurovision Song Contest was won by Izhar Cohen and the Alphabeta with 'A-Ba-Ni-Bi' on 22 April. The UK came eleventh with 'The Bad Old Days' sung by Co-Co.

On 26 August, Pope John Paul I succeeded Pope Paul VI. However, he died soon after on the 28 September.

Keith Moon drummer of the Who died of a drug overdose on 7 September. He was just 32 years old. The rest of The Who continued to tour without him replacing Moon with drummer Kenney Jones.

On 7 October the soundtrack from *Grease* became the number one album. The movie starred John Travolta and Olivia Newton-John and produced many charts hits.

Nancy Spungen, the girlfriend of Sid Vicious, was found murdered in a New York hotel on 12 October. She was just 20 years old.

Pope John Paul II succeeded Pope John Paul I on 16 October.

1979

Sid Vicious stood trial for the murder of his girlfriend, Nancy Spungen on 2 January. He was released on bail after pleading not guilty.

Lorry drivers took strike action on 5 January. Petrol stations across the country had to close due to a lack of deliveries.

On 6 January 'YMCA' became the Village People's only number one hit in the US. It later became a gay anthem.

On 15 January rail workers took strike action for twenty-four hours which was followed by thousands of public-workers striking. It was later called the 'Winter of Discontent'.

Sid Vicious was found dead in New York of a suspected heroin overdose on 2 February. The case against him for murdering Nancy Spungen was closed by the NYPD shortly after.

Trevor Francis signed Britain's first £1 million football deal to play for Nottingham Forest on 9 February.

On 12 February a thousand schools closed after a heating oil shortage due to the lorry drivers strike.

On 17 February 'Parallel Lines' by Blondie became the number one album. It featured the hit singles 'Hanging on the Telephone', 'Picture This', 'Sunday Girl' and 'Heart of Glass'.

On 17 March, Nottingham Forest won the Football League Cup. They beat Southampton 3-2 at Wembley Stadium. Forest's goals were scored by Garry Birtles (2) and Tony Woodcock. Southampton's goal scorers were David Peach and Nick Holmes.

On 4 May Margaret Thatcher became the country's first female Prime Minister. She stayed in power until 1990 when John Major took over the role.

Elton John became the first western musician to perform live in the Soviet Union on 21 May. He played eight shows which lasted for two hours each. Clips of the shows appeared in the documentary To Russia With Elton.

On 17 July Sebastian Coe set a new world record for running a mile. Altogether, he broke three world records during 1979 beating the 800m record, the one mile record and the 1500m record.

Michael Jackson released 'Off the Wall' on 10 August. It featured the hits 'Don't Stop 'Til You Get Enough', 'Rock with You' and 'She's Out of My Life'.

The first Sony Walkman was marketed in Japan. The portable machine, which took cassettes, soon became incredibly popular all over the world.

On 27 August Lord Mountbatten was assassinated by the IRA. He was killed while on board his boat at Mullaghmore in County Sligo, Ireland.

Manchester City paid £1,450,000 for Steve Daley, the Wolverhampton Wanderers midfielder, on 5 September.

Throughout 1979 the hunt for the serial killer, the Yorkshire Ripper continued. Peter Sutcliffe was finally arrested in January 1981 and was later convicted of the crimes and sentenced to twenty concurrent sentences of life imprisonment.

In November, bank rates reached an all-time high of 17 per cent.

Anthony Blunt was named as the fourth man in the Cambridge Spy Ring on 16 November.

Rod Stewart's 'Greatest Hits Vol 1' became the last number one album of the decade on 8 December.

Celebrity quotes:

'*Football is a game of tomorrows.*' Geoff Hurst.

'*I am the greatest, I said that even before I knew I was.*' Muhammad Ali.

'*I did everything by the seat of my pants. That's why I got hurt so much.*' Evel Knievel.

'*I wish I knew what I know now before.*' Rod Stewart.

'*I don't think a movie today that captured all the things that we did in the seventies could come close, because it's like asking to recreate the seventies and the audience sensibilities and that's impossible.*' Paul Michael Glaser.

Acknowledgements

Thanks to Sharron Davies and Paul Martin for their memories of the decade. Thanks also to Alan Tait, Ellen Tait, Tina Cole and Tilly Barker.

Photo credits: The author's collection, Christopher Noone, Klaus Hiltscher, Arthur Edis, Stephen Johnson, Vin Miles (Smartsetpix Flickr), Paul Wright (Flickr), Vicente Zorrilla (vicent.zp Flickr), NASA, Allan Warren (Wikipedia), Akinom (Wikipedia), Koen Suyk (Wikipedia), Evan-Amos (Wikipedia), Spring days (Wikipedia), Aq42 (Wikipedia), Esa Sorjonen (Wikipedia), Stephen Foskett (Wikipedia), Charles01 (Wikipedia), Welkinridge (Wikipedia) and Wikipedia (public domain).

Bibliography

A 1970s Childhood by Derek Tait (History Press 2011).

Nice to See It, To See It, Nice: The 1970s in front of the Telly by Brian Viner (Simon & Schuster 2010).

The 1970s Scrapbook by Robert Opie (PI Global Publishing 1999).

Cars We Loved in the 1970s by Giles Chapman (History Press 2013).

Index